*"He felt empty and without emotion.   He could
not remember when he had ceased to experience.
He could only remember controlling his feelings.
He had never allowed himself to love."*
G. Pasha Turley

cover photo

G. Pasha Turley, M.A., teaches art and photography at Southwestern
College in San Diego, California. She has also taught in Europe and has
received many accolades for her work including a Fullbright grant,
California Arts Council grant, and a San Diego Emerging Artist grant.
Her work has been exhibited in many galleries and museums internation-
ally.

WWTMMA?
(Who Was That Masked Man Anyway?)

A collection of vivid vignettes on growing up
by
Kenneth Byers, Ph.D.

ISBN 0-9619040-4-6
Library of Congress Catalog
Card number 92-53341

Published by

P.O. Box 1254 La Mesa, CA 91944

I wish, to thank Carol,
for her tireless battle,
against, my love affair,
with the comma.

gotcha!

and

To Hawkbait,
(whom you will meet later)
without whose love,
devotion and detachment,
this work might never
have come to mind.

TABLE OF CONTENTS

INTRODUCTION

To *feel*, to know what is *emotion* and what is *opinion* is always a challenge for us as men. The anecdotal format used in this book has allowed me to momentarily explore these two perspectives without depending on a lengthy novel or scholarly discourse to make a point. The following stories contain numerous thoughts I have heard hundreds of times from men all across America. They represent the meat of what men sense but cannot touch; want to say, but often just can't--to themselves, their friends, and to the women in their lives.

Each thought is presented in a way that somehow metaphorically represents an element of masculine experience encountered during my past years of studying and talking to men. For literary effect I have taken the liberty of presenting these stories from a first person perspective. They are, in fact, all representative of my own experiences; the important thing is that every man who reads them, will have had experiences similar to most of them. We know what it is to be either a father, son or friend. We have all loved and lost, loved and won, and sometimes never known the difference. Hopefully the men reading this book will connect with a part of themselves that they often do not encounter; the part that truly and deeply feels both the immense joy and the intense pain of masculinity which are inseparable parts of the experience of being a hu-man.

For every woman who reads these pages, there can be found many secrets about how men feel and why we do some of the seemingly bizarre things we do. You will know them when they appear, for many of the women who have read early versions have expressed their own familiarity with the subject matter. Few men, on their own, will ever tell you the thoughts expressed within these pages, but every man still breathing feels the colon wrenching, stomach twisting agony implicit there. Man or woman, you may note that you have also had experiences common to those you will read about here. How often we forget that we are human beings first and sexual beings second. I hope there are some reminders here.

Many of these stories were inspired from memories of my own youth. The title, **"Who Was That Masked Man Anyway?"** was itself inspired by the famous line that closed the western classic "The Lone Ranger" on both radio and television for the better part of my youth. Symbolically it represents both the mystery and heroic quality of the father in our lives. But it also represents the unknown masculine self that has contributed so greatly to the violence and dysfunctional relationships that are pervasive in our current culture. That dysfunction is found in both men and women, for, it seems to me, neither gender can know what to expect from a man when the man has no historical sense of self--no live connection to his past or ancestry. In fact, that lack of sense of self has become a common negative link between men and women at nearly all levels of relationship.

We are a culture without myths, without stories, with songs that deal with the transitory, with few poets and human values, without a verbal trans-generational art form to tell us who we are. A large percentage of us don't know our grandfathers' first names. Our rites of passage have a tradition less than one generation deep, often dependent on violence and dictated by our culture rather than responsive to it. As men, we cannot know who we are without knowing who our fathers and grandfathers were. Our stories can help us locate them. This is more than a book of "short" stories. In its larger context it is a crying out to a larger idea. The idea of being recognized and valued as part of a continuing, working culture with some kind of positive future.

I have attempted, often, to introduce the subject matter in a humorous light.   Life without laughter seems not worth living...even when the subject matter is not very funny.

AUTHOR'S NOTE

These stories were written over a period of several years with no original intent to edit them into a book. They are my thoughts and observations about many things, stimulated by many diverse happenings. Many of them came as entries in my personal journal. Sometime after the idea came to me to put them into book form, I became aware that a secondary message was being generated from the writing process. Crossing into my own middle years, many things seemed to change for me. As I work and talk with men who have spent their first thirty-five or so years, I see the same recurring sense of new awareness, of a need for self-examination that I experienced. It is the appreciation for this sense of examination of life that became the secondary process of the writing.

When I started writing my first book, **"MAN IN TRANSITION, his role as father, son, friend and lover"** in 1987, I knew I was just beginning a great new life experience. Had I any idea then of what that experience was to be like, I would probably have bought into a multilevel water filter company instead. Often during these past six years I was sorry I hadn't. The wonder of the unknown is that often we don't know exactly what to fear so we follow our dreams and try things out with only naive creativity to direct us. Looking back, however, I could simply never have dreamed the reality that has been my experience of these years of working with men. I have witnessed tremendous breakthroughs in men's awareness during the last few years. More and more men are going to conferences and weekend retreats and workshops to find out what exactly is going on, and becoming concerned about the voids that exist in their lives. We do not feel emotionally comfortable with women, children or other men. Thank God we still have our dogs.

I would hope if I have done my job well, that through the reading of these pages, men will understand they are not alone in their fears, thoughts and desires. I hope they will see that the things they have always thought about saying but didn't, or couldn't, were not weakness of the individual personality but cracks in the universal structure of the masculine foundation of self-awareness. I would also hope that they can find the self-empowerment that is available through expression of feeling and emotion, and the power that is inherent in the seemingly simple stories of life.

I would further hope that the women reading this book will make an even greater discovery--that we are, in fact, different in many ways; To honor those differences builds strength on both sides; One of the true gifts of womanhood is to nurture life, and that gift only begins at childbirth; Understanding the age-old archetypes is only a small part of the answer. We must begin now to develop new archetypes that fit new realities in a rapidly changing world. **Who Was That Masked Man Anyway?** is about men and a few of the things that happen to us; short moments of experience that in one way or another are universal to our gender.

The renowned Spanish philosopher, José Ortega y Gassett claimed that until a man reaches middle age, very little of value can happen to him. I would be hard pressed to agree with him today, but his point was that until man enters his middle years, he rarely takes the time and effort to examine his life. Perhaps he was thinking of Socrates' statement "the unexamined life is not worth living" as he wrote on middle age. Today a sizable portion of men in America are what we would call "middle-aged." Tomorrow, as we live longer and stay healthier, there will be even more of us.

Much can be given to the young man from the middle-aged and older man. Much can be given from those of us who grew up with parents who survived the great depression; who remember three wars, each altering the destinies of mankind; who remember when space belonged to Buck Rogers, when the west belonged to Roy Rogers and no one ever heard of Mr. Rogers and his neighborhood; a time when dreams were exciting; when we actually knew cops who were our friends and went to schools that were safe places to go to learn good things.

These lessons, however, are not in our laws, social directives or judgments. They are in the stories we pass on, the stories of the lives we have lived and things we have seen. In these pages I have tried to pass on some of what I have seen as a middle-aged man who has had his share of both the good and the bad. I hope that these stories will stimulate other men to share their lives with those younger men who so desperately need help to find the strength it will take as they become middle-aged. Given the state of today's world, it will be tougher for them than it was for us. I am sorry for that.

Committing one's life to men's issues is not an easy thing to do. Men have still not developed the mass consciousness of need or political base that was the hallmark of the women's movement of the 60's, 70's and 80's. We have not fully agreed that there is a problem, or even formulated the questions completely. We are, however, sneaking up on them. There is light ahead.

Being familiar with both Gestalt and Jungian psychology, I am overjoyed to see the advent of what is being called the "Mythopoetic" movement spring up around the work of such men as Robert Moore, Robert Bly and Michael Meade. The problem became clear to me early on, however, that to gain meaningfully from the intent of the movement, one needs to be rather well studied in mythology and the concepts of historical metaphor in order to really understand the mythopoetic message. For José who works days in the 7-11 and studies accounting at City College at night, mythopoetics is a tough read. Mythopoetics does not heal his pain and his desire to know something more about his own sense of masculinity. He is facing social and emotional roadblocks that he can't see, but knows intuitively. He cannot find solace or direction in the woman's movement and yet longs for the sense of hopeful self-realization that seemed to be available there for women. He must seek understanding of both his masculine and feminine essence but he does not want to make it a life study.

We are a largely homophobic society and our culture has not made it easy for men to explore their feminine side. There is a well-defined separation around homophobia (fear of same sex relationships) even in the men's movement. The majority of straight men still do not see their gay brothers as fighting the same problems and concerns that they are. Heterophobia (fear of opposite sex relationships) is experienced by gays and straights alike. However, due to the unique character of contemporary Western culture, homophobia is not, and has not been, as deep an issue in the feminist movement. For many women, the power of masculine homophobia is an area which they simply cannot grasp.

I raise the issue of homophobia because this, like many of the emotional issues that plague the modern male, can only be dealt with through emotional expression. This factor and many others having to do with the evolution of our culture and the impact of the audio-visual media, has created what has long been referred to as the "Male Mystique." The majority of American men wallow in it but have no idea what it is.

I would suggest to the reader that men are as much victims of our society as women are, just in different ways. We have both been subjected to dysfunctional family structures and debilitating media role model development. There are no longer valid excuses for the continuation of these types of destructive behavioral patterns that serve to continue the "Male Mystique". Unfortunately, because of the continuing acceptance of these factors by the population, supported wholeheartedly by the mass media, this "Male Mystique" merely perpetuates the system.

My experience in working in men's issues has brought me to some interesting conclusions. Intellectually, we are just beginning to figure it out. Once we get through the intellectualizing and discover there is nothing to figure out, we will really begin to move forward.

I do not see that the male mass consciousness has yet developed the emotional or spiritual sensitivities to deal with our ego image and self-esteem considerations. This is not a gender exclusive problem. The goal is the working of both genders, in joint effort. Women can march and aggress and hoot and holler till the Pope embraces Planned Parenthood, but until they begin to support men in their personal growth, we are in for rocky relationship travels. One great gift that women can offer men is an understanding of the power and magnificence of their feminine aspects. I agree with Robert Bly that a woman cannot ever initiate a young man into manhood--that must be, and can only be done, by an older male. But I also believe that a man must be, and can only be, initiated into his "lover" through the experience of his own feminine self. Until that initiation occurs, man cannot love himself. Until a man loves himself, he cannot truly love a woman. The paradox is that there is little in the way of initiatory opportunity available for men in this culture.

I have listened to many gurus of every conceivable persuasion from mirrored pulpit to grass-stained Birkenstocks, tell me that we are all fruit of the same tree. Well, perhaps, but I am not so sure. Years of talking and listening prove, at least to me, that men and women are, in fact, quite different. I see that we cannot look at our problems with a "one size fits all" healing mentality. The cellular biologists tell us that at microscopic levels the cells of male and female tissue vibrate at different rates. The genders cannot be anything other than different. Anyone who has ever been in a relationship knows that men and women use the same words but do not speak the same language. One can know from a ten minute walk in any woods that God knew exactly what She was doing during the creation. Man and woman were made differently because that is the way She wanted it.

The great lesson of life, if there is one, might just be to recognize and honor the differences between us. Instead of trying to make equal that which was never intended to be equal and can never hope to be equal, let us consider another possibility. *If we can learn to honor and support our opposites in their strengths and weaknesses, we can only end up with a greater whole when joined.* Two of the most outspoken and creative thinkers of the women's movement speak to this "gender" movement. Years ahead of her time, Betty Friedan in "The Second Stage" and Gloria Steinem in what some have called a "born again" perspective in "Revolution From Within" deal with this idea. I deeply suspect that Gender Studies will eventually replace Women's Studies and Men's Studies; that couples will begin to seek understanding together rather than separately, thereby unmasking the current separatist therapeutic concept which has proven largely ineffective. The critical point, it seems to me, lies in the development of awarenesses that allow men and women to understand that we are different and yet the same in a larger sense. In this way only, can we develop the gender empathy that is ultimately responsible for positive working relationships.

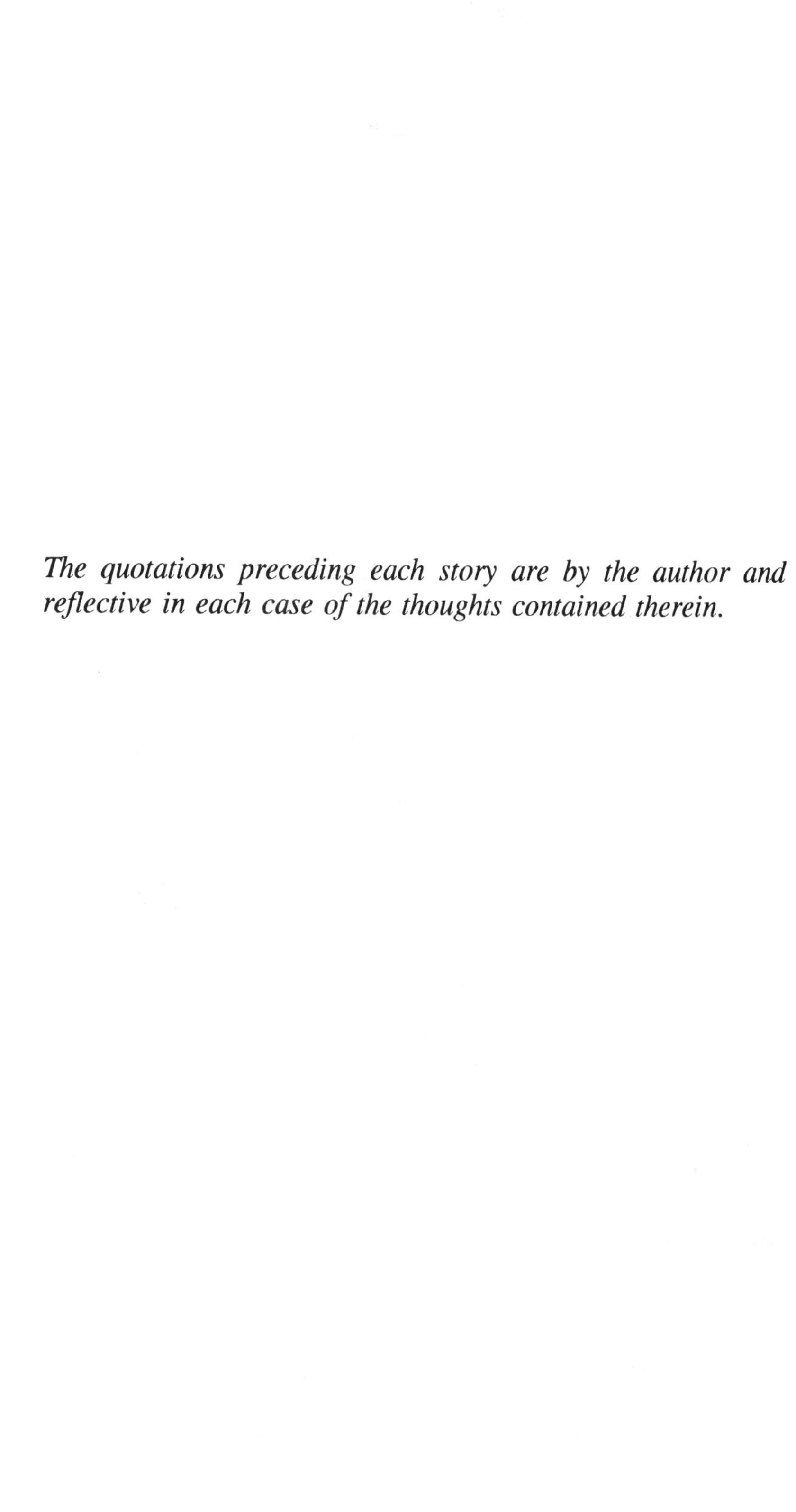

*The quotations preceding each story are by the author and
reflective in each case of the thoughts contained therein.*

It is said that if you ask a man how he feels,
he'll tell you what he thinks.

Please honor that.

What I think is important to me
and often telling you that
will teach me what I feel.

DADDY'S DEAD

The trauma came in 1949,
tho I didn't know it for
thirty years more.
1949, when the sides of cars were
made of the oak's heart
and his heart exploded.
He was fifty-one
and I was eight
or twenty or sixty-five

I was not there.
nor have I ever been,
except for sometimes,
like now.
He was a giant
simply too big for me to comprehend,
so big he did not exist.

I was walking the top bar
on the old swing set at Aunt Zelma's
when the motorcycle came
with the telegram,
we had no phone
just chickens
everyone cried
except me.

I did not cry for thirty years,
and when tears came they were empty
tears like glass balloons
sliding down a bobsled shoot
Did he ever really exist
or was he like the stories
I told my friends?
Not really lies,
how can one lie
about what he doesn't know?

Will the lie ever become truth?
Will the truth ever catch me
in the wind of life,
or must I too die to be free?
Will I be the rider of the motorcycle
for my sons?
Will they see me as I am
or will another
ride for me?

THE GLASS EYE

It is often said that as men we are just grown up versions of who we were as little boys. I've thought a lot about that lately as I begin to believe that I'm finally growing up. I think there is a lot of truth in the idea. The problem with thinking about that possibility is that then we have to remember who we were as little boys, and for a lot of men, that is not much fun. Of course, there were always wonderful parts of our childhood: the amazement at watching airplanes fly or puppies at play; the presents on days of celebration; the first roller coaster ride; playing in the streets as the summer thunder showers turned the gutters in front of the house into a torrential river; discovering that there was actually something inside a fire hydrant.

But then we must also see the other side; the one that lives in shadow. We call it our shadow self. It's where the pain resides, where today's doubts and fears were born. We don't like to go there, and for good reason. I, like you, have such a place. I did not intend to go there but I find that as I look back on these stories, I must. There have been too many triggers here, too many memories disturbed, too many doors opened.

I feel strongly that as men, we are challenged at birth to forever carry our fathers with us. For far too many of us, father did not meet our needs when we were boys so the unmet needs persist throughout our lives. Father is a double mystery; as much to us as he was to himself. He shows up somehow in nearly everything we do, and we will repeat his life, in some way or another until we deal with him. For some it is not a bad trip.   Some fathers were wonderful and loving and expressive and supportive and as a result we probably are too. But for that great majority of us for whom "father" wasn't the highlight of our life or who was missing physically or emotionally, there is usually a long battle to be fought.

1949 may sound like a long time ago to those under thirty-five. I don't find it that ancient. I was ten then, in the heart of my childhood but close enough to the end of it to have a sense that something else, perhaps even more magical than being ten, lie ahead. Dad died about that time.

Those of you who were born since the late fifties might be surprised to know that the world's leading authority at the time, for simply everything, was the Reader's Digest. Really, I'm not kidding.   Each month it presented the gospel, according to the editors, for the women of America to run their lives and families by. I would guess, more than a few men too. Yes Virginia, men read back in those days. The problem was that there were as many differing opinions about everything then as there are today. Basically, what one knew, depended a lot on which issue of the Digest one read last.

Well, apparently, the last issue that Mom had read before dad had his heart attack, (it seemed like she never missed one and devoured it from cover to cover) contained an article that was intended to help families deal with the loss of a parent. In July of 1949, the reigning wisdom read that it was best to spare the child all visible memories of the departed parent.

I was spending that summer on my Aunt's farm some eight or ten hours by train from home. It was arranged that I would stay a week or two longer than originally planned so that I could be spared the funeral. In fact, by the time I arrived home two weeks later, the house, based on the Digest's wisdom, had been stripped clean of every single memory of him, every photo, every memento, every thing that had been his...everything...I thought.

One day, some time later, while on my semi-monthly tour of Mom's chest of drawers, hunting for God only knows what, I came upon a mysterious looking blue container about the size of a watch box. I can see that box now as clearly as my hands upon the keyboard. I remember looking at that box for a long time, somehow not wanting to open it, but knowing that I would not have found it had it not been ordained somewhere in heaven for me to know its contents. I opened the box and there, to my utter disbelief, staring up at me as though I had discovered King Tut himself, was an eyeball. Trembling with fear, my sensitive young fingers reached out to confirm that it was made of glass. I knew instantly that it was his eye; but how could it be? He was...he had...holy moses, what confusion! It stared back at me for what now seems to have been hours. I put the eye back after carefully inspecting it, closed the box, covered it back up, closed the drawer and ran like hell.

My room was on the second floor and the triangle that was formed as the pitch of the sloping roof met the floor became my closet. To one side of the closet was a small door that gave access to the crawl space. This was my special space to disappear to when I needed to be alone, which I recall as being often during those times.

It is more than a little eerie summoning those moments from memory. I sat for a very long time in that dark space, not crying, not feeling, not knowing what to do or what to think. The vision of that eye ball resting like quivering jelly on my young soul. That is where I learned to deal with pain, to stuff my emotions.

Every moment of loneliness I have experienced in my life has brought me back to that moment in time. We all have had a moment in time when we shut down, when we learned not to feel, when the Digest couldn't help.

Eventually, I couldn't stand it anymore, and confronted Mother. Yes, she said, it was my father's eye, and I was never to touch it again. (Years later I learned he had lost his own eye when a passing train shot a cinder into it.) Of course, the next time I searched for it, it was gone. I never did see it again. It disappeared, just like he did.

Life went on and as I grew, I thought about the eye from time to time. I probably dreamt about it many times. Most men have a memory of their father that above all others is the picture frame through which we see him. For many years that eyeball was my father. It is only in recent years that I have been able to resurrect him as a complete human being, part by part, bit by bit, and come to grips with his memory.

It was this process of remembering, of factual and symbolic restructuring, that made me realize how tied we are to our fathers, and how impossible it is to make sense of our own lives without him.

Remembered fondly, with anger or hatred or not at all, he is us and it will always be so.

Just once,
it would be nice
to have my feet washed.

HIGHWAY 94

The bumper sticker ahead said "PRAY FOR ME, I DRIVE HWY 94". 94 floats along now under my beat up '80 Suzuki 650 as I pray for myself, for the bald rear tire, the chain stretched to the max and ready to disintegrate, taking me with it...and then there's the California drivers--all of them asleep at the wheel. A smile comes to the corner of my lips. Suddenly I find myself laughing like hell, forcing the endorphins out of my brain and into my body, releasing, releasing, releasing--laughing so loud under my helmet that tears come and tickle down my face causing me to laugh harder yet, fogging my visor in the cold morning air so I can't see a thing. Then suddenly I think, "what the hell does this puppy have to laugh about?"...47 years old, unemployed, over-qualified, 20 grand in debt, divorced with two kids to take care of. One down with the flu, the other following the Grateful Dead around the world selling tie-dyed tee shirts.

It's April, my youngest, the one with the flu, is a non-smoking musician. He's living with a friend who smokes 80 packs of cigarettes a day. He's in the eleventh grade. I'm on the streets of San Diego today having just been evicted from the apartment. I would have declared bankruptcy but I can't afford it. I don't know where I'm going, but there is enough gas in the tank to get a little lonelier. Dad, the role model, to Grandmother's house a-going.

It's raining now on Hwy 94...in southern California, where it never rains, but has been for two solid weeks. I pissed away a small fortune, learning to know myself. I feel healed but I'm not sure of what. I've found spiritual rebirth in the discovery of my own "power"...but I'm scared as hell. I feel the rain finding those openings into my body that only rain and wind can find. My boots are soaked. It's cold. Now, even the tears are cold.

The newspaper picture will show the twisted mass of flesh and metal pancaked against the bridge abutment. The pretty young paramedic, the one with the tight jeans and great tits, on her way to her first call out of training school, will throw up when she sees my pecker hanging from the spokes of what once was the front wheel. What kind of experience must it be to hit a bazillion tons of concrete on a bike at 140 miles per hour? The bike swings south onto the interstate toward Mexico. The traffic gets lighter. I twist the throttle and open it up to 75, 80, 85. It only takes a second or two. Ah, there's the bridge up ahead. 90, 95. The adrenaline is pumping its last hurrah. Man, this is going to be somethin'. Splat! Scrunch! Yukk!

I guess it was the thrill, the pure soul level choice of coming so close that made me realize I was having too much fun in the process to actually kill myself. Or perhaps it was running out of gas at 97 miles an hour that did it. I stood alone along the edge of the highway, staring down at the easy rain as it hit the pipes and steamed upward with a gentle hiss. My body felt lighter than it had ever been...safe...thrilled to be alive. Knowing that my life had changed in an instant and that I had nothing to do with it changing, I suddenly understood what surrender was. I felt my masculinity in a way that I had never known before; in a way, I felt sure, that only another man would understand. It hurt that I had no other man to share it with, to explore it with. I wondered at that moment that had there been a woman to hear my story, could she have understood the lonlyness, the emptyness. Still, I was very happy to be alive.

It is hard to walk among the roses
without catching a thorn.

ON THE STREETS

Homelessness--don't knock it till you've tried it. Then knock it. I guess it doesn't really matter why or how but there I was. No home to go home to. It was like a bad dream. Not exactly a nightmare because, looking back, there seemed to be very little emotion about it. It just kind of happened and I felt helpless to stop it. No work, no savings, no rent, and one day it was over. There I was with only a motorcycle, a sleeping bag and a few clothes. It was simple. A few days with a friend here, another there, a few nights in the park. I look back on it today, years later, and it seems to have happened to someone else. I suppose in one way it did. I think we are all schizophrenic in one way or another at various times in our lives, and this was one of my times.

It was a time of pure reflection. It was February in San Diego. Even though it was cold at night, I suspect that any homeless person anywhere in the country would trade a week's food for a bus ticket to San Diego in winter. If you gotta be homeless, this is the place to do it. I don't drink or do drugs so there was no part of the experience that was lost or insignificant. I remember it all, but it shows up like one of those pictures that are all fogged up around the edges for effect. Almost romantic in a sick kind of way.

I've never tried to write about it before. It is not easy. My journal notes don't help much. I do not have the ability or the desire to reconstruct the sadness and loneliness of those moments in today's words. And yet, it was in some ways the most powerful three months of my life. That is not a recommendation to anyone to recreate this experience. Please do not try this at home.

Life on the streets is an interesting duality, the ultimate social paradox. It is everything you know and are familiar with, but it is also foreign and frightening. There is a comradery, a commonality among thieves, that is the support system of the streets. But don't trust anyone. Death and pain are only a blink away. There is only desperate survival available. Like tigers in the jungle, there are jealously guarded territories; certain corners for philandering; certain doorways for passing the nights; certain unspeakable initiations of the subculture.

Lost souls, lost minds, properly known as Ronald Reagan's legacy to social responsibility, most of these people simply had no place else to go. I don't blame Reagan. He saw that we couldn't have Star Wars and adequate mental health care at the same time. It was not his fault, simply a matter of priorities supported by a codependant society. The American people let it happen. The American people are still letting it happen.

I was able to get out because I was able to deal with the issues that put me there. I am very fortunate. Most are not. The under-educated, the out-of-work, the 'Nam vets, the mental patients too sick to function "normally" in society but not sick enough or well insured enough to take up a hospital bed, the victims of our self-strangulating governmental bureaucracies, the hopeless and the addicted--these are the street people. They are now becoming a political force just through their sheer high visibility. They are also becoming bolder and louder.

I look at the phenomenon of homelessness as prophetic of the battle for men's awareness. It might even be seen as a metaphor for the world condition. There is the same social malaise, the same mass resistance to responsible action. Homelessness might have been a suitable war cry for men's liberation a few years ago, but now there are too many women and children out there. One need not look too hard, however, to see that they are still mostly men.

The metaphor I speak about can be seen in the eyes. Those men do not share the reality that society holds as lawful and righteous. They are fathers and sons who have no connection with their own fathers and sons. It is not a problem of low self-esteem but of no esteem at all--no sense of who they are.

The name of the game is much the same with many men, it is just a matter of degree. Only the characters have been changed and no one is protected.

I have been on both sides of the soup kitchen line. Being served and later, as things got better for me, serving. I am beginning to understand the meaning of the word "Brother".

Once I figured out
I wasn't Humphry Bogart,
and John Wayne died,
I had to face myself.

I didn't pass.

AT THE MISSION

The sun rose over the burnt orange tiles of the mission roof. It was a Tuesday morning in early March, and the dew danced and sparkled joyfully along the tops of the perfectly manicured grass. My sleeping bag was damp with the fresh smell of the night's perfectly distilled tears. The sound of the morning rush hour was beginning to express itself on the Interstate just a few hundred feet away. I had been sleeping there for about two weeks and I had no doubt as to why San Diego has such a large homeless population. It is simply a wonderful place to be homeless. Besides the generally pleasant weather, you can be very much alone and no one really bothers you.

The long subtle slide from successful entrepreneur to street person had been painful, exhausting and yet interesting, in a totally disassociated way. It had taken two years, a divorce and who can count the number of crises, large and small. My life had been whittled down to a motorcycle, a bed roll and a few clothes. I was making enough money to eat and my friends let me use their showers. I had a number of offers for a room, but it was clear to me that living on the streets had a certain message for me and I needed to listen. It was a good place to simply be alone, for the first time in my life.

I thought a lot in those days about my old college reading heroes Woody Guthrie, John Steinbeck and Jack Kerouac and how they found so much beauty and value on the road. Even if I was thirty years late, I wanted a part of that insight. I knew that there was a part of every man that dreams of doing what I did. Giving it all up and hitting the roads, hopping a ride on the freights or hitching to Malibu with two wonderful young blondes just looking for a guy like me to play with. But the world has changed a lot since the romantic surrealism of the great novels of yesterday. From the perspective of the streets one can easily see that few of us really care anymore about much of anything, outside of our own creature comforts.

I stood in line at Father Joe's kitchen for Thanksgiving dinner with some 800 other homeless tourists and ate my fill of tradition. I sat for endless hours in the park downtown listening to the tales of horror from vets who killed people in ancient villages with funny sounding names. Guys who came back whole but totally fucked and had the gift of a V.A. hospital to fix it. Guys who were not fond of Ronald Reagan. Black men who dreamed of winning the lottery and living in a big white house on a hill. White men who dreamed of a bottle of wine that would magically never empty. Women who just couldn't face another pregnancy, another beating, another trip to the county home to see their kids...and those who brought the kids with them.

Often, I felt I really didn't deserve to be there. I hadn't really paid enough dues to know these people on their terms.   I hadn't felt enough pain, enough hopelessness, enough end-of-the-ropelessness. They knew it. I didn't make many friends. I was never black enough to be black or white enough to be white. I was a visitor. I had something they didn't know they had--choice. But they sensed that I had it.

On this particular Tuesday morning, I woke up to a brilliant and warm sun peaking over the mission roof edge like Kilroy in a 1940's poster. I knew, as my eyes opened slowly to let the world in, that I had made my choice. I had learned what I came to learn and it was time to go. By the end of that day, I had a job, but there was little victory in it. The life I had been living was all a lie, but it was required experience.

The loneliness that exists in the living of the lie of life is the essence of the masculine experience. It is a lie that is all too familiar to men who have had to mold themselves around the media-generated idea of masculinity. We lie because the pain of truth is too great. We lie because in the depths of our soul we fear the world will discover we don't fit the mold. It is the haunting reality of a life of not knowing who we are, and why we are here and who we are trying to please and why.

It wouldn't be so bad if we weren't so sure we needed to know.

I am my father's rage,
and if I don't heal that rage,
my sons will be
their father's rage.

WHO WAS THAT MASKED MAN ANYWAY?

God she was big. I remember mom looking down at me and screaming, "just you wait till your father comes home...he'll teach you to tell lies." Apparently I already knew how to tell pretty damn good lies or she wouldn't have been yelling at me like that. But the fear of those words was so great that it didn't really matter. I don't know how old I was, but mom was four feet eleven inches tall and she looked big as hell to me, so I couldn't have been around too long.

Dad was a big guy, about six feet tall. Now if I thought four-eleven was big you can imagine what I thought about six feet. I don't actually remember dad ever hitting me. He didn't have to. He did this thing called thumping. It might be illegal now. He would press his index finger against his thumb and flick the finger at the back of my head with amazing force. His thumps held the terror of the ages. I learned early not to mess with father. I didn't need to worry about it very often because he wasn't around very much. Mom was not capable of much in the way of discipline and I think I had figured that out by the time I was three.

Dad fished most summer weekends, hunted in the north woods in the fall and winter, and worked five and a half days a week. Evenings we would all sit around the living room radio and listen to the news with Lowell Thomas and then the Lone Ranger before bedtime. Then he would usually disappear into the garage to work on the boat or his fishing rods or something. In any case all those things were definitely off limits to my inquisitive young hands. Those hands earned me many a thump as a youngster.

I remember a surprising number of things about those years. Born in 1939, I remember air raid sirens and blackouts; half moons on the headlights of cars; playing postman with the food ration stamps; the horse drawn truck of the junkman who sauntered up and down the streets singing out his desire to collect the neighborhood cast-offs in some unrecognizable language; the old glass milk bottles that would freeze on the doorstep in the bitter Detroit winter and push the little paper cap two inches above the top of the bottle. The milkman, the postman and the bus driver were heroes, men (always) who could be trusted to do the right thing. A kid could count on the same ones being around every day for years. They always knew the names of every kid on the block. I remember Sonja Henie ice skating, life without television, and Saturday afternoon at the movies for a nickel, two full-length cowboy features, ten cartoons and a Superman serial. For a nickel! But I don't remember much about dad. Mostly, I remember him as a disciplinarian. I know now he loved me more than life itself and I think I even knew that as a kid. But it was love from a considerable distance. Usually the length of an arm with a thump on the end of it. He died when I was about ten. I remember wondering at the time if he figured I was getting too old to thump and he just wasn't needed any more.

He came and he went. He was a mystery to me. I never knew who he was and yet, I knew everything I needed to know about him. He was my father and that was enough. Although he was never far behind me, I didn't really think about him too much. Until, that is, one day about twenty five years after his death, when in a fit of angry reaction to one of my sons, I thumped him. That completely spontaneous reaction, long hidden in my unconscious, caused me to stop and look at how many other ways I reflected my father. Was I, too, a mystery to my boys? Did I, too, make myself so unavailable to them that they saw me only as a disciplinarian? Did my father's rituals become my rituals? The answer to these questions was of course, yes.

In every episode, as the Lone Ranger rode off into the sunset we heard the same velvet throat ask the question. It was like watching it through a frosted window pane, as we each saw a symbolic part of our father and of ourselves, riding off on that blasted white horse. As much as we wanted him to stay, all we could do was stand there helplessly and watch him go.

All those years I was growing up I had asked that question about my own father; "Who Was That Masked Man Anyway?"

I found out.

He was me.

*To see the world through
the eyes of a child
is to know God.*

GONE FISHIN'

Most adults forget that a week is a significant percentage of the life already lived for a six-year-old. That's how long I had to dream about goin' fishin' with my Dad for the first time. Finally, he had said, I was old enough to go with him. After all my sister had already gone and she was only five years older than me and a girl besides. The week was an eternity, and I'm afraid my whining, pestering and impatience made it even longer for him.

I recall the mystical nature of the seemingly dozens of rods with the brightly colored teeny-weeny little bands of color on either side of the chrome-plated little roundies that the fish line went through, and which were also perfect for holding dandelions; the reels upon which said line was so carefully wound, that clicked with a musical clatter when the line was pulled; the cute little hooks that I craved with unabashed obsession to play with and never could under threat of having my hands bound palm to palm until they grew together (it hadn't been too long since I swallowed the safety pin at the dinner table); the boat that hung with lecherous temptation from the ceiling of the garage, just beyond my most inventive climbing abilities, which God knows was unmatched in my neighborhood; such delights as nets and ropes and scaler and pliers and boots taller than me and hats with stuff hanging all over them, worn only for fishing and an unending number of wondrous little things that only God and my Dad knew about.

And then there was the tackle box. Oh my, what wonders of other worlds, what unbelievable and magical sorts of things resided in that old black metal box. To have been able to get into that box would surely have made me the happiest boy the world had ever known. Unfortunately, Dad knew how powerful were my intentions, and kept a nasty old padlock on it. Everything in that garage smelled of or looked like or was destined for...fishing.

You see my Dad's whole life seemed to revolve around fishing. How anyone could sit for hours in a boat, at anchor, and wait for an innocent little fish with limited intelligence to bite a plastic worm is beyond me even now. But then...ah then it was quite a different story. The unknown was magical and drew me totally into its web.

Well, the week finally went by and it was Saturday morning. Long before the sun rose he came into my room and woke me, dressed me as I stood like a limp slice of celery, not fighting him but certainly not being of much help. I slept through breakfast and the long ride to Lake Michigan in the cold spring morning darkness, except for short occasional bursts of consciousness to ask if we were there yet. By the time we got to the lake I was hungry. We slipped the boat into the water and set out for what was surely to be the adventure of my life. I imagine it must have been around six a.m. by then because I can still see the sun rising over the water in my memory. It might have been the first time I had ever seen that because it left a deep impression in my memory. We motored out a ways while I munched on a sandwich or something; and then a piece of fruit; and then a piece of bread; and then another piece of fruit. By the time we got to our fishing spot I had consumed all of my rations for the day and was cautiously eyeing his.

He stopped the boat and just drifted quietly for a while, my eyes fixed on him. He sat and looked at the water and listened to the wind. Soon he decided on just the right spot and went about getting everything ready. I recall the seriousness of the effort to him, the ritual that accompanied each movement. I was, many years later, reminded of the moment while sitting through a Japanese tea ceremony. Each thing done just so, everything in its place. He knew exactly what had to be done. I watched in adoring awe and fascination until, finally, we were ready to fish. As I watched, he skillfully strung a squigalling worm on my line and dropped it into the water. He smiled, bent over and handed me the pole. Then, with the artful grace of a ballet dancer, he stood up and silently stretching his rod behind him, cast it forward, propelling the fly on the end of the line easily twenty miles out into the water. Slowly and quietly and with practiced patience he would reel the line in and then repeat the process perfectly, time after time, ad nauseam.

Just sitting wasn't much fun for me. I learned in rapid succession what one does not do in a boat while father is fishing: One doesn't move around, talk above a whisper, pee in the water, drop things in the water, play motor boat in the water, whistle, go swimming, play cowboys and indians (one could do that in those days without running afoul of the A.C.L.U.), ask endless questions, or tell stories. About the only thing I could do was eat. As a particularly precocious child, I learned all this in the first few minutes after anchor drop. Fishing, I was sure, was fun but after five whole minutes and no fish, it was getting old...and for some reason, father didn't seem to be having much fun either. I wondered why all the fuss about just sitting quietly in a boat... quiet was for sleeping. I may also have done some of that, I don't remember. I don't even remember if we caught any fish, but somehow I can't imagine *him* not catching any fish! I do remember, however, Dad finally telling me, with some disappointment, we would be home for lunch. Although I had planned to be out fishing the whole day (as I am sure he did - he never came home before dark), the thought of eating lunch at home seemed to be O.K. I finished his sandwich on the way and slept the rest of the trip.

It is said that understanding passes from a man to his grandson because they are both closer to spirit. To the son, father is rule-maker, a disciplinarian, a force to be reckoned with, a challenge to manipulate and get past, a source of inner fire, a guide to the warrior self; grandfather is wisdom, gentleness and surrender. But every once in a while, as fathers ourselves, or with our fathers, we have a moment in which there is a deep connection, a recognition that although doomed to conflict, each generation is responsible for the life of the next. We have a connection to father that is limitless in some dimension whether we understand it or not. I cannot pass a fish laying in a supermarkt display case without reconnecting with my father at some level.

Whether it happened, in fact, as I remember it or not is of no importance. I remember it as I have told it, and it gives me strength to see his face once again as he threaded that worm on my hook. From where I sit today, it takes a lot of love to put a worm on a kid's hook.

I do not know when I became a man.
It all seems fuzzy.
Nobody told me.

OF BAR MITZVAHS AND GOLDEN IDOLS

Having been brought up in the Jewish faith, I had, by the age of thirteen, long looked upon the Bar Mitzvah as a time of major importance. This was, I remember thinking, as I trudged to Hebrew school each Tuesday and Thursday afternoon in the cold New England winter, a significant rite of passage. All the crap had to be worth the presents and money in store for me. To learn to read Hebrew, which of course would get me nowhere that a bus wouldn't, one needed to have rabid motivation. All I had to do was get through it and the relatives would all come through with golden idols, and then, I guessed, I would be a man.

The relatives were always asking, "so when does this child become a mensch?" To become a mensch (man) is a unique mystery to a twelve year old. I always wondered what kind of schmucks these people were. They knew that for centuries a Jewish boy hits manhood at thirteen. Everyone knew that. (I felt particularly good since most of my friends were Catholic and I got to be a man before them, I guessed...only God knows when a Catholic kid becomes a man.) The adults didn't need to know that when I first masturbated, at eleven, was when I figured it happened, but no one gave me the golden idols for that. Even so, I must confess to having had a certain insecurity about manhood.

The day of the Bar Mitzvah came and went. The suit that Mom bought me was worn maybe three times before I grew out of it. The watch got lost in a couple of months. The Hebrew went in six days. The bucks I got sat in the bank and grew at a big three percent a year. The money was gone before I finished my first year of college. The idols were gone by thirteen and a half mostly. Only the masturbation remained. I remember the Rabbi talking to me about the responsibilities of manhood. About how I would be viewed by my peers and elders in a new light. It never quite happened. I may have passed a ceremonial milestone in a traditional sense, but it sure didn't reflect in my reality. I was still just a kid popping pimples and doing everything possible wrong. It left a hole of mistrust of both myself and the whole idea of manhood that stayed for many years.

When do we really know that we have become men? What happens that is different than yesterday? And why doesn't it happen to all of us at the same time? In native cultures since time began, there have been rights of passage that were clear to all members of the society. At a certain age each boy went through a ceremony to anoint him into manhood. But then he was able to hunt, to marry, and to provide common effort for the tribe. Today we have no such opportunity to know when we pass into manhood and to have that passage validated by the culture.

Getting the driver's license, graduation from high school or college may help. Marriage or military service can help. Fatherhood should, more often than it does. I often hear women complaining about the fact that men are immature long into adulthood. Women don't seem to have the problem. I think it has to do with the fact that when men separate from mother as children, we have few role models to follow into manhood. Mostly the men are working or otherwise missing in our culture. Women know that motherhood brings passage.

Even for those who don't have children, there is a recognition that when they are of an age to do so, they carry a responsibility that men cannot relate to. I think that we, as grown children, cannot know when we become men without spending some deep ritual experience in the process of transition. We must first find the need to want to know. We must deal with the little boy inside who doesn't want to leave but knows he can't stay.

He's the one who gives up on the relationship because he doesn't understand how to make it work.

He's the one who gets lost in drugs and alcohol and self-abusive behaviors.

He's the one that cannot stop the rage that violates those he loves.

He's the one whose mind shuts down and closes out the world, because he doesn't know how to become part of it.

Most of us just go from one Bar Mitzvah to another gathering the golden idols.

I have been unable to find the manhood there.

THE HOT DOG MAN

Sometime during the late sixties the amusement park in New Haven became condos. I had graduated college and moved to Pennsylvania by then but I never forgot the summer nights walking the boardwalk "lookin' for babes." There was simply no greater time to become a teenager than the early fifties. No civilization before or since in the entire history of the universe will ever have that opportunity to live American Graffiti. None ever had a better time.

Actually the amusement park was a bummer. It was just a place to run '49 Mercs and '36 coupes against the latest technical brilliance from Detroit. We had genuine leather seats, wrap around windshields, lowering blocks and purple dots in the center of the tail lights. What more could a guy ask? If he couldn't get laid, (that being a rare enough happening), he could carry his love affair with the automobile into history.

But there was one other thing about the amusement park that I will never forget. I received an important initiation into manhood there. It was there that I discovered what commitment and dedication to purpose meant. *It was the Hot Dog Man.*

I think his name might have been Frank but it's not important. He worked at Jimmies. Jimmies was world famous for its hot dogs and fried clams.

Now I must say a bit about the fried clams here too. We are not talking the wimpy little ulcerated, undernourished, rejected strips of inedible and less digestible leathery insignificance that the world now knows as fried clams. These were New England's own precious secret. The whole mass of juicy and bountiful protein, complete with full intestines and often sand, rolled in a secret batter and fried to various levels of perfection in rancid lard. The large order was 75 cents. It came in a box like the one from the chinese take-out. It comfortably fed two hungry teenagers stressed from hours of cruisin' for babes, with only a couple of good stories to show for it. Unimaginable gastronomic delight!

Actually I almost never ate hot dogs, except of course, for Miccalizzi's in Bridgeport...his whole stand couldn't have been as big as a Fotomat drive-in store. He wrapped each dog in a strip of bacon and grilled those suckers till they screamed.

There was always a line there and his daughter was a knockout, but that's another story.

In order to get the clams we had to stand in a line that formed at noon and stayed at least fifty people deep till 2:00 a.m., seven days a week, spring, summer and fall and weekends all winter long. That line wrapped around the building and followed the counter to the order station for the last ten minutes or so. This is where Frank (or whatever) did his thing.

Basically, Frank flipped the hot dogs...but with a speed and accuracy that would render Mohammed Ali speechless in his best days; with a slight of hand that would cower David Copperfield's magic. There is no doubt this guy could have out-drawn Clint Eastwood on any day.

One could stand and watch this hyperactive obsessive-compulsive wiener flipper until hypnotized into a lobotomy-like state. On a steaming hot grill, sweat sizzling and popping as it dropped from his forehead to the hot grill, this modern folk hero performed his act with relentless bravado. Armed with a razor sharp knife, the blade now a well ground sliver of its original state, and with his left hand, he would slice and flip, slice and flip, move, adjust, slide, twist, slice and flip, all in hyper-seconds. Never did I see him touch the grill with his fingers. Rocking back and forth, shifting his weight from foot to foot in orchestrated rhythm, he would perfectly process maybe a thousand hot dogs an hour and no one could figure out how they ever got into the roll. He was that good!

It was here that I learned that no matter what a man did, if he did it to the very best of his ability, he would make his mark. Frank was a major mentor in my life and he never even knew me. Mentoring in our culture is all too often an accident. There are many things a woman cannot teach a young man. He must learn them from an older man. I never needed to learn to flip hot dogs, but I did need to learn that every hot dog is important. One never knows who's watching. I think that as men we must realize that we are constant role models to the boys who watch us. We must always be aware that we are teachers, and just that awareness will help to make us worthy.

Frank, I'm sure you're long dead of a heart attack, but just in case...I want you to know you made a difference.

Sometimes
I cannot tell the difference
between the little boy inside,
and the man in the mirror.

THE PEEING TREE

When my first boy was an infant, I had a friend with a son about four. We lived in the same apartment complex which backed up to a golf course. Late one summer afternoon I happened to see my friend and his son walking across the open green expanse toward a huge old Oak tree. I parked and watched them, thinking about the day when I could walk with my own son, and teach him of the world. When they reached the tree, each unzipped his pants and proceeded to urinate on the great old tree. When they finished they zipped up, turned around and headed back across the fairway to their apartment.

A day or two later when I happened to see my friend, I asked him about that incident. It was a beautiful story which I will share with you.

As a boy, let's just call him Bill, Bill did not have much physical or emotional contact with his father. The man worked a great deal and it was not the kind of job to which he could take Bill. So Bill watched Dad disappear six mornings a week to some secret place, with great curiosity and not a little jealousy. His Dad worked very hard and when he got home it was his habit to have a quiet dinner and listen to the news on the radio, tuck Bill into bed and disappear again, to where, Bill had no idea.

On Sundays Dad would spend most of the day wrapped around the newspaper or sleeping, or doing a little work around the house. The father didn't talk much to Bill and by the time Bill was four or five, he had learned that Dads were not very available for conversation. There was never much doubt in

Bill's mind that his father loved him very much, but he could never seem to get the same kind of attention that Mom gave him, and it bothered him. Wasn't he, after all, a man, just like his Dad?

So, at around the age of seven, Bill decided that he needed to talk to his Dad. One bright summer Sunday, he approached the older man and asked why he never talked to anyone but Mom. Bill asked if that meant his father was not happy, and if his unhappiness was Bill's fault. At this, his father stared at Bill for a few long moments. Slowly, the father took Bill's hand and walked with him in silence to a far corner of their property. Here they stopped beneath a great old Oak tree.

"Son," the big man said, "there is no greater happiness in the world than in this old tree. It does not have to talk to be happy. It is happy just being a tree." "But you are not a tree, you're my Dad, said the boy." "Yes, but knowing that you are my son makes me just as happy as this tree." The boy thought about this for a moment, looking up into the full and inviting arms of the tree. "But Dad," he said eventually, "how do you know the tree is happy?" "Well", he said gently and with a rarely seen smile, "we can tell by the great size and fullness and richness of its branches and by its strength." "Can I help the tree be happy?" asked the young one.

With this, the father thought for a moment. "I'll tell you what Bill. I'll bet that if you give the tree a gift, it would be even happier than it is now." "What kind of a gift could we give a tree, Dad?" "Well, the most important thing for a tree is water. Without water the tree would quickly die. Suppose you and I pee on this tree and give it the gift of water." "Oh yes, cried Bill, let's do that. Let's do that."

After that day it was never very hard for Bill to find a way to talk to his father. He would just ask him to come pee on the tree with him. Bill does not recall his father ever refusing.

With the passing years and the life of his father, Bill forgot about the ritual. Life got complicated, he fell in love and was married and eventually had a son of his own. That afternoon, when I had seen the two of them at the Oak, the boy had asked his father a very serious question. He wanted to know the difference between boys and girls. Bill felt uncomfortable but hesitated to brush the query aside. Suddenly, the memory of his father came to him and he took the boy into his first initiation. As they stood before the great Oak, Bill told his son, "the main difference between boys and girls is that girls can have babies, which is very nice. But boys can pee on trees."

*Why does the counting stop
after the money's counted?*

MEN AND MONEY

I was married for a long time--twenty-three years. In some parts of America that is just about unheard of. But we stuck it out as long as we could, and then we just grew apart. Both growing but in different directions. We had two kids along the way.

I worked hard, building a business so that my family could have all the things they needed and some of the things they wanted. I did a pretty good job. But somewhere along the way what I wanted got all mixed up with what everybody else wanted.

The drive to provide, to be considered a "successful" husband and father got confused with being emotionally available, to myself and everyone else. I felt incapable of doing both. My wife complained that we needed more money so I worked harder and then she complained that she never saw me. My kids needed more time from me as they grew older and I had to make more choices. There were times when the money was tight and coming home meant having to say "we can't afford it." So sometimes I just didn't come home.

There was the time my wife went looking elsewhere for the love and attention she didn't get from me. She thought it meant I didn't love her. I loved her enough to forgive her. Somewhere, however, deep within the bowels of my confusion, I was beginning to boil over with resentment. It all seemed to have to do with money. It seemed that I was an OK guy when the providing was good, but lost my value as a person when things got rough. My picture frame through the eyes of all those I loved was made of money. It was a classic double bind that is familiar to every man alive.

When the women's movement came along I thought, Great! Now women will learn what it's like to carry the responsibility that men carry. It is truly no greater or lesser a responsibility than that of women, just different. A difference that appears to have gone largely unnoticed. It is still a rarity for a woman to offer to pay the tab on a date. There is still the expectation that a man's job is to take care of the woman. The courts still almost always award custody of the kids to the mother and order the father to pay. I was lucky. I got the kids. The kids were lucky too, but we didn't have to go through the courts. There was a great fairness in it in a way. She gave them what they needed in the early years and I was there to give them what I could in the later years.

But it is not only about the kids. There is an enormous anger between men and women. By the time most women today reach their middle years, they have been through at least two lousy relationships with men. Often one of them was with her father. It usually leaves them with a significant trust issue. Trust becomes in large part the major issue because very few men can ever hope to meet the expectations of the average woman caught in her own trust bind. It's not her fault. It came with the plumbing.

Many middle-aged men prefer dating younger women. They are a lot more fun, for a while anyway, and usually a lot less angry. When a man has to deal with an angry woman, it brings up every negative experience he has ever had with a woman. The older the man, the more bad experiences. When a man brings up a trust issue in a woman, it brings up every trust issue she ever had with a man. Very often, just being a man is enough to bring up the issue. It's a wonder that men and women ever stay together at all.

Anyway, back to my story. Eventually I made a lot of money and could buy a lot of things. My wife went to work and made a lot of money too and we bought a lot more things. Boy, we really collected the things. But I had accessed her anger through the tough years and she had learned not to trust me as a "provider." She had accessed my anger equally, and there was a part of me that, try as I might, knew no forgiveness. We were never able to reform the kind of partnership that we had in the early years. Too bad. It was a good one, but we didn't know it then.

Since we parted, we have both gone our separate ways on somewhat friendly terms. The expectations she has of me as a friend are the same ones she had of me as a husband. I don't know why I would expect them to change. I also don't know how I can fulfill them any better. We have both spent a lot of time getting rid of all the stuff we collected together. Most of it is gone now.

We are each beginning to collect our own, new stuff. Our own money...and we both spend a lot of time searching for someone to share it with. Someday perhaps it will all make sense.

THE MEN'S GROUP

In my occasions to speak before groups about men's issues, I often ask the audience what it is they would most like to know about men and men's issues. Almost always one of the first responses is another question: "What are men's issues anyway?" I would like to address that with a story about what is rapidly becoming a major component of the men's movement of the 1990's.

It was a small Arizona town which, because of its particular scenic beauty, drew mainly women and fewer men from all parts of America. Many came to pursue their inner quest for spiritual peace, understanding and perhaps gain some glimpse of wisdom. I had lived there about half a year and experienced some of each, except the wisdom which was somehow devilishly elusive. The decision to form a men's group came one summer day at the local watering hole where a few of us had stopped for a couple of beers one hot, sultry late afternoon.

The four men I was with, all of us in our mid-forties, were climbing buddies, finding masculine pleasures in foraging paths to the tops of the mountains and mesas that erupted arrogantly and seductively from the valley floor and laughed at us tauntingly from 800 or 1,000 feet above. We had been climbing all day and were exhilarated but exhausted in that wonderful musky way that confirmed our manhood to all who would care to notice, and many who didn't.

Someone had asked why we risked our lives just to get to the top of something bigger than ourselves. It was a thoughtful question which led to many others, equally as troublesome.

Troublesome because we had no answers and, as any woman knows, a man without an answer is indeed a wretched encounter. It all started innocently enough when I suggested we all go back to my place and talk about the climbing experience.

The five of us settled down in my living room, and as we talked the conversation began to shift from good times and bold experiences to the fears we each experienced as we moved up the mountain that day. Within a short time, we had gotten into the deeper subject of fear itself and how difficult it was to allow ourselves to accept the reality of feeling afraid. As the talk extended through dinner and into the night we began to discover that each had experienced fears that he thought only he had felt. It came as a distinct surprise to find that the other guys felt the same things. We talked long into the early morning hours and finally broke about 2:00 a.m., exhausted but filled with delight at our new found experience. It was the first time that most of us had ever taken the time to talk to another man about anything other than work or sports, and we all loved it.

We ended by agreeing to continue the talking the following week at my place. It was the first meeting of a men's group that was to continue for just over a year until two of us moved away at about the same time. We met without failure every Wednesday night for two and a half hours. We added a few other men and discussed every conceivable subject that had anything to do with men. It had no real structure and we tried many different kinds of things. Two of us were in the psychology field, two were artists, one business owner, one gay waiter, and a doctor. We laughed, we cried, we told the truth to each other. For each of us it was the very first time we had ever been able to confide and trust in another man.

We talked about our fathers a lot. About how we didn't have any real idea who they were. About how they seemed to have no connection to anyone outside themselves and about how we longed to be hugged and accepted and loved by them. We worked through many issues around women. We worked at trying to figure out what women wanted from us, and what we wanted from them. Why we needed them as wives, mothers, friends and teachers and gave so little in return. About how we were frightened of, but somehow connected to, those men who loved other men. We got to explore our addictions and our myths about our own masculinity in ways that gave us pride and compassion toward ourselves and other men.

We explored our visions or lack of them, the need to cry but the immense resistance to it. We helped each other walk through the pain and loss of a relationship, the death of a parent, the loss of a job, the birth of a child, the failure of a business, the unfolding of a new relationship and the agony of a divorce. We asked questions and dealt out discourse on our spiritual connection to God and to each other, the meaning of life and why we needed nuclear war, recycling and Buicks. And yes, we even talked about sports...but not for long and not very often. We talked a lot about violence against men and against women, about the fact that 95% of all prisoners are men, and that most women are angry as hell at men and we hadn't a clue as to why. We spent a lot of time together, this group of men, and we loved each other a lot.

That group has drifted into many corners of the land, and each of us has started other groups and seen many groups grow and develop as ours did.

When I'm asked now by someone in a group about what men's issues are, few have any idea why I laugh and why a tear comes to my eye. But you're learning.

*Most of all
I want to be loved for who I am,
but sometimes
I try to be
what you want me to be.
It is not always
the same.*

MAGIC LADY

It was without question something out of a supermarket novel. I stood against a wall watching slides of a friend's travels abroad. There were perhaps a hundred people milling around in quiet respect, sipping champagne, exchanging pleasantries, testing and judging the catered munchies. Suddenly, I became aware of a strange, macabre, presence. An unidentifiable energy sweeping around me. I looked uneasily around, saw nothing and resumed my state of reduced metabolism. Within thirty seconds I felt a woman standing next to me. I was not aware of her arriving, only her presence. Not just any woman this, but a most remarkable woman. I noticed my heart beating.

I saw her through the haze at the edge of my field of vision, as my pulse began to pound in excitement. Tall, blonde, strikingly beautiful with an animal magnetism of volcanic proportion. Dressed by her own personal Goddess. For an hour, or perhaps five minutes, we stood next to each other in silence, each waiting in barn burning expectation like a couple of kids for the slides to be over, yet dreading the responsibility of that moment to connect. She occasionally would look past me, on her left, through the glass doors into the spectacular night view of the city from our mountain top perch. As she did so, I would also, that our gazes would not meet and ruin the expectation. I would occasionally look past her, on my right, to the entrance of the room, to casually judge the latest entries therein. Her magnificent head would turn in involuntary motion, in perfect rhythm, in the same direction. All I could see was the glow of her perfect blonde hair seductively intermixed with the natural brown. Occasionally a whiff of scent would reach out and attack from her elegantly sloping neck and totally immobilize my olfactory system. Our eyes never once met during that year we stood in anticipation like five year olds waiting for the doors of Disneyland to open. Then it happened. The lights came up and we stood motionless, each waiting for the other to make a move. With my insides exploding and imploding simultaneously, I turned and said something perfectly stupid, like "don't I know you from someplace?"

In fact we had met before. About two years prior she reminded me...professionally. We had spoken for a few minutes, fatally attracted then as now. My interest then was sabotaged by the enormous diamond ring on her wedding finger. My ego bludgeoned into silly putty by her canary yellow Corvette, parked hauntingly next to my very basic, small, motorcycle. But I had kept her business card. It kept appearing in the random flow of papers on my desk from time to time...like an immune fungus.

The conversation started. We babbled aimlessly and fell hopelessly into each others eyes. It was all I could stand to not tear her clothes off and offer her to the Gods as Nirvana incarnated. She asked if I knew a particular minor celebrity in the room that she wanted to meet. I lied, and asked if she would like to be introduced. I wasn't aware I had lied. I wasn't even aware I didn't know him. It wasn't important. I just took her hand and guided her over the clouds to him for the introduction. As our palms met our souls welded together. The twenty feet of time space along the physical journey became an eternity of knowledge. He, as minor celebrities often do, feigned our long standing friendship, not really sure if he had ever known me or not. The conversation was short and polite, and not one of the three of us heard a word of it.

She was an artist and I asked if I might come see her work. She accepted. At five the next afternoon I made the first of what was a forty-five minute drive to her parlor of sin and passion and joy and white light. A drive I would make uncounted blissful times during the following two months.

She was, of course, still married, although miserably so. She was, of course, confused, beset with guilt, ravaged with conflicting feelings. It was beautiful. It was intense, powerful, intimidating, empowering, wonderful. And always impossible. It was the most wonderful experience of my life. It ended as quickly as it began and with the same amount of warning. I never knew why. I pray that I'll never find out. It seems that to explain it would somehow rob it of its magic.

Herb Goldberg in his book "The Inner Male", talks about the magic Lady syndrome. He must have known her. She was my Magic Lady and I was her Magic Man. We came together in the nuclear center of the mass of creation. Neither left the same as we entered. Someone once said, "all love must end in pain." I know that to be truth. Even the pain was wonderful. "It hurts so good," as my chiropractor would say.

I still think of her from time to time. In a way, I will always love her. We brought to each other, in my fifty first year of life, in her forty-ninth, a gift of knowing that passionate, meaningful romantic love can be had at any age. It is not the exclusive right of the well tanned hard-bodied youth, on whom I sometimes think, it is all wasted.

Life is such a gas. Just keep your eyes open and a toothbrush in the glove compartment. You never know.

The Marines build men.
I was never a marine.

MEN, VIOLENCE AND WAR

There were thirty men in the social room of the church. They had come together as they do once monthly to discuss issues of interest to men. This night the subject was "Men, Violence and War". America and the world had just entered into the saga of Desert Storm.

For two and one-half hours we expressed our feelings. Given our location in a major Navy port, many of the men were ex-military, some currently active. One brought his not so recently retired officer's uniform replete with braids and medals. He spoke of the symbolism of the uniform. Others spoke of violated boundaries, the probability of genetically programmed masculine violence, a country trying desperately to heal the wounds of Vietnam by proving that we could, after all, do it right. There was anger from those who had fought in past wars and hated themselves for the killing, and remorse from those who hadn't fought at all and hated themselves for not having killed.

There was talk of love and fear and pride in America, and a lot of concern that a lot of young boys were going to die on both sides of Bush's line in the sand.

But that was last night, and today the war is over. Life will now come back to normal. The nation's adrenaline will settle down and the returning heros will spend their time polishing shoes, walking tall and remembering the war that brought back to each of them a bit of masculinity. Even for the solder girls. As I think back to that meeting and what was said in a roomful of men who desperately cared what was happening in their world and, as I see the troops drifting back tomorrow and tomorrow, I can't help but feel that we've missed something.

I think it's called friendship.

Watching the TV tape of the surrendering Iraqis, I began to get a sense of it. At those moments these men were not violent, angry fighting demons. They were each a father and a son of someone who loved them. They were hungry and tired and wounded within, in ways that only show in the eyes. Believer or infidel, there was a moment of connection as they crossed that line that could not be denied as brother met brother in the craziness. Those men wanted desperately to be held. They were all little boys then. They just wanted it to stop hurting.

I see it in the prisons in the men I talk to there. I see it in the men who have crossed unspeakable boundaries that violate the rights of others in cruel and sometimes desperate ways. There are moments in the lives of most men, when we cross the violence barrier. When we loose control of those social definitions of "normal" reaction. When we wound not only others but ourselves.

We become greatly defensive when our little girls are abused and molested as children, but somehow it seems OK to abuse and molest our adult children, mostly boys, by asking them to kill and be killed. Why don't we see the violations there? But there is more that we don't see.

Men don't generally have many close friends. That's why we demand so much of our women. They have to be everything to us, including our friends. But in war, we get to have real friends. Our buddies are our lives. Literally. We form bonding under conditions of stress that make life bearable. We get to have friends. Perhaps that is one of the reasons it is so hard for us to let go of war. We can even be friends with our enemies in war. In a perverse kind of way, there is always a bonding that occurs in an adversarial relationship. That's not always true in our normal lives. Many men can go for years by themselves, without friends. Until the next war.

Could one hope to suppose that if men could find ways to have and be friends, I mean real friends, not back slappin', beer drinkin' buddies, but talking and caring friends, that we might not have to have any more wars? That the men might not have to send any more boys (and thanks to legislated equality, now girls) to die for them? That we would not need to express ourselves in violence? That we could find our American pride in American virtues instead of Patriot missiles? I would hope so.

I was once told in an encounter training that there is no hope. Well, maybe, but I think I'll hold onto mine for a little while longer, just in case.

There is an important part of me
that is a warrior.
The world
does not make good use of warriors.

THOUGHTS ON WAR

I sat and watched, spellbound, as most of us were. The TV ablaze with the hypnotic repetition of the war so far away yet right there in the living room. It was not a war like wars used to be. This was a silly war. Two heads of state, playing a deadly game of "I bet my dad can beat up your dad." And yet, still it is the young boys who die, sent to die by men. The poet Robert Bly asked that question; "Why is it that it is the older man's job to send the younger men to die in war?" The real name of this game was "I bet my kids can kill your kids."

The interviews said it all. The boys and now the girls, proud as hell to be part of the greatest killing machine ever created. We can only guess at the real power of what we have wrought with our trillions of dollars in tax money. But the hints are there. Those fresh young faces, well-trained, well prepared, ready to...kill. We should be proud.

But did you notice the fear in their eyes? The tentativeness as they repeated the government issue rhetorical response to the press who endlessly asked inane and pointless questions to fill up their bylines because everything else had already been said a thousand times and more.

Then, there were the generals. They sure looked spiffy in their desert camouflage dress. (The British generals even had matching undershirts, Bill Blass no doubt.) The men were calm, confident, precise as they talked about the day's work. No feelings, no opinions. Just the facts. Some things never change. Where the hell was John Wayne when we really needed him?

As one watched the shots of troops at work, it was difficult to tell the boys from the girls. They worked well together. It was obvious they respected each other. I saw them both as boys, however, because our men had sent them both to war. I had no such problem telling the men from the boys. It's the boys who die in this game, not the men.

I had to wonder what would happen if there was a rule in the game that only men over forty could play? It would probably never sell.

And what about when it's over? What will the men do when the boys on both sides are dead? When the women and children who stood watching wide-eyed and hollow as the bombs erased their cities, suffer the pain of grief, disease and deprivation, while the leaders play "say uncle."

Will the arrogance and righteousness of the men who decide the fates of millions know the wounding that humanity suffers in the name of liberation? I don't think so. Their concern is not the young boys. Their concern is winning the game. Only the game counts.

I think the men who play the games have no idea that it is not a war of right against wrong, or high principle above barbarian power struggles. It is a game of men who have forgotten that the boys learn from them, as they learned from their fathers.

When will the fathers say it is time not to kill the boys?

When will the fathers say it is time to learn something new?

The bond between
mother and child
can never be broken,
it can only be incomplete
by degree.

The bond between
father and child
must be nurtured
to exist at all.
The chances for failure
are infinite.

MUSIC MAN

It's been a very long day. Up at 6:00 a.m., write for a couple of hours, work all day, do some errands and run a therapy group until 9:30 p.m. Now it's 11:30 and I'm standing in a smoky bar, but I neither smoke nor drink. At 51 I'm easily the oldest person here. My saving grace is that I don't have the shortest hair.

The wonderful young girls pose with delicate security to see who that good looking kid at the other end of the bar is staring at. Two hundred or so pair of eyes darting about, afraid to land anywhere for more than a few seconds. When they see it's not them being looked at, they light up a cigarette. They don't even notice that I'm taking it all in, in my best Hemingway-like tradition.

The band is so loud I can feel my pulse keeping time. It is a small college area bar, that brings in new local bands to try out. My kid is up there on stage in day glow trousers that in other times might have been a hot air balloon. His Guitar singing out in rhapsodic harmony to the monotony of a reggae beat. Incessantly. I hate reggae. I see no comparison to music in it at all. And yet, this group is good. I find myself mesmerized in the rhythms, delighted in the joy and happiness of the kids on stage and off. The beat of the music is everywhere. Every nimble young body, and a few not so nimble, moves to the beat...even mine. Everyone, somehow, in some mystical way, is connected.

I feel a great sense of gratitude that these kids can find a moment of pleasure in their music. As I look around, I fall swiftly into a time warp and for just an instant, remember myself, 30 years ago, in a bar just like this, when I did smoke and drink, and the length of my hair wasn't all that important. It was not meant for me to make the music then, although I would have battled lions to be able to. It is my son's turn now, and I get to share two dreams. Mine and his.

Suspended momentarily in my time travel I heard the music of Presley and The Beatles and Jefferson Airplane and The Yard Birds. Just as loud, the same insecure wonderful girls, the same lost young boys. I'm struck by how little has really changed. The years flash by in period syncopation. I think about what it would be like to do it over again, starting here, tonight and it seems for a moment like a nice idea. I am sure that the girls in my bar never looked as good as these here tonight.

Finally, the smoke gets to me and I have to leave. As I walk out the door, I become aware that I smell like an old Pennsylvania Dutch tobacco barn in the fall. The cool night air brings me quickly back into the Tuesday evening. I am thrilled that my son gets to live through all this from under the lights. I am delighted that he can and am proudly jealous of his talent. I look forward to sharing his experiences. But all in all, I think even if I could, I wouldn't want to do it again.

Once is enough--but there is great merit in the dream.

*I went to a bar last night
and bought a light beer.*

Nothing happened.

*My friends didn't lift me up
onto their shoulders, my team didn't win,
and I walked home alone.*

HERE'S ONE FOR THE BROOKLYN DODGERS

The day Adolf Hitler decided irrevocably to march on Europe, Mom marched on Woman's hospital in Detroit to deposit a new incarnate on the planet. In all my eternal wisdom, I didn't have the good sense not to return. I think I remember coming in wanting to do a little bit of everything. I know I came in wanting to play baseball, but I was looking in so many directions that my eyes crossed.

I actually remember Dr. Spiro at four. (I was four, not Dr. Spiro) I actually remember the operation, I swear. Mom told me years later that I had the first successful muscle shortening eye operation in history. Thanks, Mom.

As it turned out, the eye was fine. But even at four, every kid on the block knew I had always been cross-eyed. Current scientific proof to the contrary, I was never to be recognized as "normal."

When baseball came into my life at about six, I was never chosen to play, because of course, I was cross-eyed. Well, never mind, me and Dad would listen to the Tigers play on the radio. He even took me to a couple of games, but I ate him out of a week's pay each time, so it wasn't often. At nine he died (I was nine, not Dad.) I wasn't interested in much of anything. We moved to Connecticut a year later, and I became a Brooklyn Dodger fan.

Uncle Sidney took me to a Yankee game once. I hated the Yankees. Sid had no kids but was determined to be my surrogate Dad. He blew it big time, but that's another story. Plus he smoked cigars. To be a cigar smokin' Yankee fan was beyond forgiveness to a die hard Brooklyn Dodger kid.

Then it happened. In 1953 the Dodgers abandoned me for some fool place called Los Angeles. I had had it. I did not go to another baseball game for thirty eight years. I would not be humiliated again.   Any kid who, like myself, faced the crushing disaster of always being picked last for the street team, also had to deal with this basic abandonment issue. We all have that one. It comes when, at age 3 or 4 or 5, we noticed that we were different than mom and psychically split away from her. The problem is that we didn't see it that way in our infantile wisdom. We thought she abandoned us. So, as you can see, the Dodgers pushed a big button for me on their way to the Chavez ravine. Besides, I had begun to notice girls.

One day, early this season, I got a call from a buddy who had two tickets for the red hot Padres and asked me to go with him. Well, I figured, I had already made just about every other mistake I could have, so I probably couldn't curse my Karma any further by going. The red hot Padres were playing the slumping world champion Cincinnati Reds. How could we lose?

We had great seats. I was only disappointed that they didn't recline. The red hot Padres lost to the slumping Reds in a 1-0 yawner. The single run came as a complete accident in the ninth. Being cross-eyed would have been more fun. Actually the highlight for me was getting out of the parking lot just seconds before the exits all jammed up.

Men very often get lost in sports, because that's where our heroes are. We can identify with sports heroes and become the instant successes we want to be through them--if only for a moment. It's the closest many men ever come to the truly wonderful sport of day dreaming. The team represents the friendships and comradeship that very few of us ever get to experience. Sport is a wonderfully available expression of our masculinity in a society in which we struggle daily to find that experience. It is good that we have it. There is a thrill of identification that follows the beautifully tuned bodies around the diamond, or down the basketball court or grid iron. When we cheer our team or boo the opponent we are acknowledging ourselves in those men. We are connecting. We are honoring the best and expressing anger at the worst of ourselves.

I have often been told by women that the thing they disliked most about their relationships was that their men spent too much time watching sports on TV. The breweries will hate me, but I believe that as men begin to experience their own masculinity on a daily level, the need to identify through sports will become less obsessive. That we have sport is perfect and wonderful. When we obsess over it, it becomes libido masturbation.

I often ask myself if I would have felt like more of a man had I enjoyed baseball. It really does look like fun in the beer commercials. But then, everything looks like fun in the beer commercials.

Nope, the truth is, I am perfectly fine having made the choice between baseball and girls.

ON MARRIAGE

Many men get married. Almost as many, it seems, get divorced. Women, too, of course. Last night I went to a gathering of a few friends who wanted to get together and talk about "things." We talked about relationships, power, love, spirituality, you know, those insignificant subjects no one really knows anything about but everyone likes to discuss-- four men and one woman. Twelve marriages, eleven divorces. I was there with my one little divorce and kind of felt like I had come to the wrong place. I felt somewhat guilty in fact, about my lonely little singular divorce and even more so that the marriage had lasted, I almost hated to say it, twenty-three years. As the evening and the discussion evolved, I started feeling worse, because somewhere down in the deep reaches of my soul I actually had to admit that I enjoyed most of those years. Well, the last three or four weren't exactly a day at Disneyland, but the rest really were not bad. One guy had been married and divorced four times. But he was a doctor, he could afford it. After a while, we all admitted that we would each love to get married again. Even the woman.

There was lots of talk and it was a lovely evening; good friends, good food, good wine, and in the end, we all left to go our separate ways.

As the road home stretched out before me I began to wonder what it would be like if there was a law that said, when you married a person, you had to stay with that person forever, and you couldn't cheat on that person. And, if you did they would cut off your ear or something, so that most people wouldn't cheat. I guess it would mean that most kids would have real dads instead of a succession of temporary "uncles." It could mean that adults would have to learn tolerance and respect and honor. It might even mean that couples could go out together and have fun. They could also go out separately and have fun with their friends, without worrying about being cheated on. It sounded like a pretty good idea to me, but I don't know if it would really work out very well.

It could ruin the economy.

It would bankrupt a lot of lawyers and single clubs filled with divorced folks who want to meet other divorced folks to get married to, who were just like the ones they divorced.

And what would a few good friends have to talk about over all that good food and wine?

Neh, I guess it's not such a good idea after all.

FRED THE SNOWMAN

The kids were about 10 and 12...the time goes so fast it is hard sometimes to remember them relative to a specific age... and they had been particularly miserable for the past two months. Christmas had come and gone, and school was happening every, single, day. The Virginia winter had settled in like an old maid aunt moving in unannounced. It felt like Moscow looked. The market was in its winter doldrums; the orders dragged in as though the final holocaust was imminent; the mailman appeared daily with the lethargic aura of a bear coming off a too-short hibernation; no one seemed to want to do much and the flu was going around. We didn't have Nixon to kick around anymore and Gerald Ford certainly wasn't much fun. Well, you get the idea. Winter in Washington was pretty boring. I needed a change of scenery. My mind had gone dead and it seemed one more day at the office would unplug me for good.

West Virginia is kind of like North Dakota, I think, although I've never been to North Dakota. (Why would anyone *want* to go to North Dakota?) Once you're actually in West Virginia however, it is a wonderful place to be. The dark mountains and viciously winding roads expose brilliant beauty at every turn. I had decided to spend a long solitary weekend in a cabin in the mountains. I just needed to get away and experience some quiet. The noise of life had become deafening and I had stopped listening anyway. I needed some time to think, to sit on the mountain top, to discover who I was and recreate my life.

The conference center was open only in summer but they said I could have a cabin if I didn't mind the fact that I would be the only one there. I smiled. The homely, overweight girl behind the counter looked at me funny as I signed in. The restaurant on the main road was open twenty-four hours a day for the truckers who still managed to find their way up the mountain for whatever reason. It was a beautiful little cabin nestled among white birch and old oaks, built in a Swiss chalet style. One large room with cathedral ceiling, a loft with a big warm bed, a small kitchen (which I stocked with a hearty selection of junk foods brought with me), and bath with a large white tub. There was no phone or TV but there was a supply of firewood for the generous stone fireplace along the north wall. I built a fire and sat back in the old over-stuffed rocker listening to the quiet. Just me, the creaking rocker and the crackling flames. I had not even turned on my car radio all the way there. I was completely alone and it was perfect. As the sun slipped unnoticed in the west, somewhere over the gray, cold, heavy air, I climbed into bed. It must have been about four-thirty in the afternoon. My mind had stopped in time and dreaming was simply out of the question. Rest was all that mattered.

There is something about the silent babble of falling snow that touches a weary soul. I awoke suddenly. There was a faint cold-gray tonality inside the room signalling daybreak. I just lay there for a few moments trying to make sense of this place; figure out where I was, how I got here, and why. Suddenly it all came into focus. I looked over at the window and noticed that I could not see out of it. It took a few moments to realize that glass was generally clear and that I should be able to see something out there. The only thing I could hear was the familiar tune of the theme from "The Twilight Zone" from somewhere deep in the cerebral reaches of my brain.

My mistake had been not listening to the radio. Had I done so I would have heard that the blizzard was expected to stop over my cabin and dump 300 feet of snow on me. Well, it seemed like 300 feet. Actually it was only about ten feet by the time it stopped two days later. No wonder they closed for the winter.

With makeshift shovels and my hands I was able to tunnel out the front door to daylight and also to the firewood stacked next to the door. It was fine with me, this unexpected imprisonment. The security guard found my tunnel and checked up on me and suggested I stay right were I was as I couldn't get anywhere anyway. All the roads for miles around were closed. So I got my wish. I was totally, completely, and wonderfully alone in this magic land of whiteness.

I set about the process of emotional rediscovery and self-exploration. I read parts of a number of books and got bored. Then I got bundled up and went out and played in the snow. Ever try to walk around in ten feet of new snow during a blizzard? That didn't last long, but I did build a snowman outside my window under the protection of a long eave that served as a storage shed. I named him Fred. I didn't realize at the time why I made him. I read some more, counted the stones in the fireplace, ate, munched, examined things, and watched the snow fall. The first day went by pretty fast and at sunset I once again found myself falling into an early sleep.

On this second night, however, I awoke at about 3:00 a.m. The snow had finally stopped and the wind was blowing around making drifting sculptures in the bright moonlight. I began to think about this process of finding myself. I had no idea what I was looking for and less of an idea of how I would know when I had found it. I spent the next two days firmly focused on these questions, discussing my thoughts, as they came, with Fred, through the window. The plows came, cleared the snow and left, the sun came out and began the ritual melting process and I had a couple of meals at the restaurant.

It was during one of these meals when the first clue came to me about what I was to discover. I was sitting at the counter talking to a truck driver from Tennessee. He asked me what a city boy like me was doing out here in the boonies, and I explained it to him. He looked at me for just a second and said with all the wisdom of a biblical sage, "Man, don't you know you can't find anything but loneliness by yourself?" I just stared at him. "I sit in a truck a day long and I'll tell you what, I don't find out a damn thing about me, or anything else for that matter, until I stop for a rest or a cup of coffee. That's when I get to talk with the other drivers and guys like you. That's when I get to see me and it has to be bouncin' off of other folks. I can't tell nothin' bout me by myself. It's like, without you I don't exist. Do you understand what I'm saying? Even if I don't like you, if you're not here for me to find that out, ain't no way I can know whether I like you or not, right?" His commentary hit home and I remembered that Carl Jung, the great psychologist, had said much the same thing. Later, after I had returned home, I looked up the exact quote:

> And there really could be no Self if it were not in relationship; the Self and individualism exclude each other; the Self is relatedness. The Self doesn't exist without relationship, only when the Self mirrors itself in so many mirrors does it really exist; then it has

roots. You can never come to yourself by building a meditation hut on top of Mount Everest; you will only be visited by your own ghosts and that's not individualism; you are all alone with yourself and the self doesn't exist. The self only exists inasmuch as you are related, inasmuch as you appear. Not that you <u>are</u> but that you <u>do</u> is the Self. The Self appears in your deeds, and deeds always mean relationship; a deed is something that you produce which is practically outside yourself, between yourself and your surroundings, between subject and object--and there the Self is visible.

I went back to the cabin, packed up and prepared to drive home. As I walked to the car for the last time, I passed Fred, stopped, and bid him farewell. It struck me as ironic that I had created Fred unconsciously to temper the very loneliness I had intended to experience.

As I walked in the house my wife greeted me warmly and the kids ran up for hugs and stories of my adventure. That's when I began to find what I was looking for.

PILOTS

At eight and seven respectively, Ron and I had been co-pilots for as long as I could remember. Together we had refought the entire Second World War from the cockpit of the most elegant, fastest and maneuverable airplane the world had ever seen.

Approachable only from the hayloft, easily the weakest and least safe part of the old barn, which, had there been anyone with the energy to do it, should have been torn down a generation earlier. Howard Hughes had his plywood Spruce Goose--we had the rotting wood, flying barn. But when you're seven and eight years old you see things in your own special way. Besides, who ever even heard of Howard Hughes?

There was a space where the shed roof had sagged and separated from the eaves at the hayloft's edge, leaving an opening that looked remarkably like the front of a B-17 bomber. (Well, we thought so.) Underneath, right next to the landing gear, the pigs snorted and grunted in the mud and straw. With crayons and paint and old boards, we labored at our artistic and scientific best to create controls and gauges and signs and all kinds of stuff with which to fly the thing. Fly we did for untold hours over those two summers. The war had been over for a few years, but we still had plenty of maps and pictures to plan our attacks with...we were the best. It was during one of these flights of fancy that Ron and I made a bond about flying. A promise to each other that no matter what, we would both grow up to be pilots. We pricked our fingers and traded blood in solemn oath.

Life, however, has a way of directing us away from our most enthusiastically planned dreams. The last time I saw Ron was the summer of 1949. Well, the last time for about thirty years anyway. After my father's death, the family moved east and we lost track of the cousins. We moved, they moved, there was no way to find them.

One night in 1982, as I sat at the dinner table with my own family, my oldest boy Brian, then twelve, asked about my father's family. There had never been anyone from my side at any family functions, because there weren't any. I was the last namesake until my boys were born. Brian particularly, was quite taken by that fact. But he was not satisfied with the missing relatives story and kept bugging me in his best twelve year-old fashion about finding them. So in one of those rare moments of divinely guided desperation, I picked up the phone and called information in Indianapolis and asked for my aunt Zelma by name. Now there happened to be a listing there for the initial "Z". That was close enough and I placed the call. She answered the phone in her best 86 year-old voice. Ten days later Brian and I arrived in Indianapolis for the reunion.

Of course Ron had gotten his pilot's license. Of course I flew United, mostly. I remember feeling strangely uneasy about the fact that I had not kept that commitment to my cousin. Ron also owned his own plane, a small Piper four-seater. On the second day of our visit we went flying. Neither Ron nor I had forgotten our pledge, but it was never mentioned. There was no need to. A bond had been broken between us that was more than just two kids playing in a barn. It was greater than and different from, the thirty years of non-communication. It was the essence of what brings trust into any relationship. We had given our word to each other in solemn oath, and I had broken the oath. It was only two kids playing, but it was really more than that. It was something that we all do many times in life. We make it OK to break our word. We find all the rationale we need to not complete. We do it as individuals, in relationships, families, governments. We make it OK not to keep our promises. There was a part of each of us that I disappointed by not learning to fly.

We were only a couple of kids playing in the barn;
but it must have been pretty important at the time.

People expect me to be a certain way.
Bosses, friends, lovers, kids, police, the IRS.

Everyone expects something of me.

If sometimes I can't perform,
I need to know that it's OK.

THE UGLIEST CAR IN TOWN

I've owned some nice cars. Some very nice cars. There has always been a certain awareness that, to some extent, I was my car. That is to say, I had always felt that because my car usually arrived before me, most folks would judge what got out of the car by the appearance of the car. I think, in America, cars have always been marketed with that idea in mind, so it is no wonder most of us believe it. I certainly always did. That is until I found "Farfeneuggin".

I'm still not sure how the Volkswagen ended up in my parking spot. I remember my son driving it for years. I remember telling him it would be a major mistake to scrape the paint off with a razor blade. I remember how easily he exposed all three previous layers of farfencolor. Actually, the four colors in their unique scraped pattern gave it a certain distinctive quality. It wasn't until he slid under the rear of the UPS truck and created the farfenpugnose that I started to worry.

One day, not long after he started college, he announced that his mother had bought him a new truck and therefore was no longer in need of the farfenugly. He wanted to take it down to Mexico and plant it along the farfenhighway. Well, several years before in a psychotic infantile rage, I had traded my BMW in on a motorcycle. After three years of full-time cycling I was considering the purchase, once again, of a car; and, having spent a considerable amount of my money on his little farfenbugger, decided it would be OK to drive it myself for a while.

Based on its visual presence, I really thought that it would run for about another week and simply melt down and disappear. Eighteen months later, despite my negligence and abusive language, the damn thing was still running like a real car. I kept thinking about "restoring" it. Fixing up the U.P.S. customizing, painting it and the like. I even got some estimates. I swear to you that Earl Scheib refused to paint it! He said all the old paint would have to be sandblasted off and it would cost about three times what the car would be worth in perfect farfencondition.

During the time I drove this doggie do-do vehicle, I was always amazed at the reactions of people. I dated a lovely lady for a while who made me park it around the corner. She always drove when we went out...I liked the sharing.

I once stopped to pick up a couple of "illegals" sneaking across the border...they turned around and went back to Mexico.

I took it in to have the oil changed once and the attendant closed the garage door so that it couldn't be seen from the street...he didn't think I noticed.

The homeless, looking for handouts, waved me on.

The Volkswagen and I developed a certain understanding between us. As long as I would drive it, it would get me where I needed to go at 30 plus miles per gallon of regular gas. I put close to twenty thousand farfenmiles on that damn thing. Most of them alone.

I think the best parts were the looks from passing women. Stopped at a light, I would look over and make eye contact with an attractive woman, who would smile back until the car came into focus. Mostly their eyes glazed over instantly. I might have been worth millions, but it made no difference. I suppose I could say that the car saved me many unhappy relationships.

It is nice, however, knowing that my real friends never mentioned it. They knew that it didn't matter to me what it looked like, and that was fine with them. As long as I parked it around the block. But I really <u>liked</u> the car. It had character. It was not another look-alike from anywhere in the world. It was a bit like me I suppose, and the uniqueness I saw through the windshield was merely a reflection of my own uniqueness.

It was my cosmic joke on the world and the world got to laugh.

And so did I.

My loneliness comes from my father.
It is deep...so deep I cannot touch it.

You can only help,
but do not find fault with yourself
if you cannot fill it.

PRIMAL LOVE

Somewhere deep within the twisted maze of arms and legs and breasts and bellies, I heard her say, *"I don't care what your name is, just tell me you love me"*.

It was at the end of a very long day on the road. I had stopped in the small Pennsylvania town motel bar to have a drink, to settle my exhausted, rattled nerves, before going to bed. I didn't even notice the empty glasses on the bar in front of the vacant stool next to me as I slid in and placed my order.

It happened very quickly. A beautiful young woman returning from the powder room, easy conversation, sad stories of unrequited love. Hers and mine. And now, scarcely two hours later, we are lovers entwined in the misty memories of how it was or might have been. Each of us drowning our secret desires in the arms of a stranger whose only real connection was the desire to be loved.

"I don't care what your name is, just tell me you love me," I heard her say. I stepped out of the steamy passion for a split second to wonder at the meaning of such a request. And then, as if there were no other option, I complied. For a few moments we loved each other with all the abandon and desire available to the human being. Through her, I loved every woman I had ever loved or wanted to love. She, through me, every man.

Afterward, as we lay silently, our skin touching and soothing wounds not expressible in this dimension, I wondered again. Why is the need to be loved so strong? What is it that drives us to express those needs in such an emotion-packed connection? In twenty years of marriage I had rarely felt the kind of release I had experienced that night. It seemed to have little to do with sex, or the attraction to the other person. It was a primal longing. A need so deep that it exploded without warning, without effort, without plan or purpose.

Every man, and I would guess every woman, carries that need within. We find thousands of ways to deny the expression, but never stop looking for an opportunity to experience it. And even when we do, it seems not to be enough. It seems always that there is something more to experience, something more to be had that we might have missed.

Someone once said, "Life is what happens while we plan for the future." I think perhaps the primal need to be loved is like that too. We let what we have go because we are so sure there is something better out there. And when we find her, we find she doesn't care what our name is.

What I came to discover later was, I do care what my name is.

And so did she.

It is easy to get lost in the world.
Those times when I can be alone are
when I find myself.

HAWKBAIT AND THE BACHELOR

From the top of the mesa one can see the entire city of San Diego tentacling northward; the amoebic expanse of Tijuana, Mexico rising into the stale brownish air; the rugged naked mountains sleeping eastward and the empty beauty of the Pacific wandering lazily westward. The immediate terrain was dry brush, sand, gravel and sage grass. My companions were two scientists from some university up in Washington state who were looking for a piece of land to dry farm experimentally. They were sure the world could be fed from ten dead, desert acres. I was showing them a property owned by a friend. As we looked into the canyon descending before us I spotted a Red-tailed hawk circling overhead, just steps in front of our location. The hawk is a magnificent bird, exhibiting great drama in its soaring mastery of the air currents, and yet something unseen telegraphs the brutality of its nature. I caught myself being hypnotized by its beauty and grace. But hawks don't just fly aimlessly. Their search is for food as they create magic on the wind. Then I heard the rustle in the brush.

I looked down and just ten feet in front of me I spotted the object of the hawk's affection. Out there in the boonies, miles away from the nearest house were two kittens, obviously of common ancestry, neither more than three weeks old, fluttering about catching thistles and weeds and feline Devas. I surmised they had been dropped off by some sad human soul to relieve himself of such dire responsibility as caring for these fanciful creatures. One black and skittish, the other a fluff ball of beige and white.

Oblivious to the danger that circled above, they jumped and played like this was just as much home as anywhere else and they belonged there and everything was just fine. I looked around and, as far as I could see, there was no sign of anyone or anything that could protect them from the hovering menace above.

Well of course I couldn't just leave them there. The very last thing I wanted or needed was a cat. The little white fluff ball seemed to understand that, and if you have ever known a cat, you know they always go first where they are least wanted. They are plugged into some multi-dimensional energy flow giving them special access to information mere humans cannot know. He found some form of comfort by attaching himself to the heel of my shoe, while the black one ran under the car and hid.

Living alone had been a joyous experience for me. I was raised with my mother and sister and moved from their house directly into another when I married my other mother. (At least retrospectively.) I spent the first forty-seven years of my life locked in the drama of living with women. My youngest son's entry into college saved me from having to spend additional years dealing with him at home. Since then, I had learned to treasure the deliciousness of aloneness. Then comes this damned cat. I found the black one a home but the fluffy one wanted me. So, of course, he got me.

I have learned a lot from Hawkbait. He is now almost full grown looking a lot like a Himalayan with thick, long, tan and white fur, sparkling blue eyes, a raccoon mask and a weird white stripe down the left side of his face, mocking his hereditary royal lineage. He is adoringly affectionate but never obnoxious about it. Hawkbait's purpose in life is to have his stomach rubbed and he will contort his seemingly totally disjointed body in any form necessary to create that experience at any time and any place suitable to him.

What I have learned from my fuzzy little roommate is first, he's a godsend for getting women into my apartment. Fortunately, I haven't run into any yet that are allergic to cats. Secondly, I have learned to share with him at a deeper level than I have ever shared with anyone. I find myself almost constantly in conversation with him. No matter what I tell him he never argues with me, never judges me. Usually he just does what he wants anyway and I have learned to love him, not in spite of it, but because of it. We sleep together and honor each other's space, yet, when he gets up and leaves to go sleep on the computer, I feel no loss or abandonment. I am 100% responsible in this relationship. There is no argument about expectations or projections of guilt. There is just Hawkbait and the bachelor having a solid relationship.

I find that I am looking at my human relationships differently now because of H.B. I have discovered what qualities work in interacting with others and it is so simple; just allowing others to be who they are, and not trying to change someone to fit my picture of who I would like them to be. I either like them and accept them or I don't. Hawkbait will be my friend as long as I do not try to force him to be something he is not. I have found that to be true of my relationships with my human friends, too. The men and women in my life, as well as my own children, are a lot like H.B. in that regard. It seems the closer I get to another human being, the more I must look at Hawkbait to see clearly what is happening. There is no question in my mind the cat knows I saved his life. These animals are full of instinctive behaviors that are a wondrous mystery to us. One thing is sure, however, and that is he knows everything he needs to know to survive. I'm the one with so much more to learn.

> *I fear getting older because
> I don't know how to change.*

TURNING TWENTY-ONE

In most states of this fine country the legal drinking age is twenty-one. It seems to me a paradox that perhaps the only universally recognizable right of passage our youth can enjoy is being "legal" at twenty-one. It is of course only symbolic, as I would guess that nearly 100% of those young men (and women) who desire to lift a frothy mug to lip have done so long before that age is reached. (In fact, an uncomfortable percentage of them are, unfortunately, confirmed alcoholics by that time.)

My son recently reached that mystical milestone of maturity. We celebrated as we have on many other birthdays by going out to dinner. Over the years, going out to dinner has become a ritual between my son and myself. He is a musician and not fond of alcohol. Being underage in a band was often a handicap for him because most of the gigs available to young musicians are in bars. So, indirectly, it was a very important day for him.

As we sat in the chosen pub waiting for dinner, he sipped his symbolic bottle of beer and I a symbolic glass of white wine. We reflected on the years that saw him grow into the fine young man he had become. I was saddened his mother could not share his day with him, she now living in Europe. He too was saddened. For the past fifteen years, as boys must do, he had spent, much unconscious effort separating himself from his mother. Although unaware of it, the genetic inheritance from deep within the unfathomable mystery of the DNA had catapulted him into his manhood, with neither choice nor control.

The past several generations have seen an overwhelming

majority of boys (and, of course, girls) growing up in separated families. My son was fortunate in that his parents stayed together until he was sixteen. Most people experience the trauma and terror of family breakup as children. Regardless of the age of separation, there is a resultant wounding and a loneliness, well hidden in the soul, that can be observed only occasionally. One such moment was in that pub, as he turned twenty-one. I have seen it far more often in younger boys. It's scary, and I feel much empathy for their sadness. It is a sadness which emanates from the initial separation from mother and carries on into their own relationships with women. The fear is one of abandonment; of being left by yet another woman. It runs strong and true in the male psyche. Even though in most instances the children go with the mother in the family breakup, the boy's masculinity goes with the father. There is no way to regain it without many years of hard work--and the boy must seek out his father to find it, either in actuality or symbolically.

Sitting there in celebration, I thought I spotted a dropping of his guard once or twice. For just an instant or two the passage into manhood that we are led to believe has something to do with age, appeared to break through the binds of the growth process. I think I saw a self-recognition and awareness of his own masculinity.

The bottom line question, of course, is does it really matter? What difference does it make when we really become men? With all the philosophical and intellectual effort expended on it, I am not sure we really ever know anyway. We have expended thousands of years on the question through story, metaphor and mythology. It has played havoc with philosophers and thinkers who philosophize and think about such things. But there is something about the reality of watching one's own flesh and blood moving into the unknown that makes me think it is important. The fear of the unknown is always greater than the unknown itself. The trouble is, we never get to really know that until after we are forced to move through the fear. We don't know we can handle manhood until we've already done it. By then it no longer matters; unless, of course, it does.

My son said twenty-one felt different than twenty, but he couldn't say in what way. Only that it felt better. I felt badly that there was no cultural rite or ritual available to mark the event. Ours is the only culture in the history of the world to become great without masculine rites of passage. It raises some serious questions. Have we outgrown the need or are we simply refusing to acknowledge it?

On the steppes of Russian Siberia, as well as in most other nations throughout history, there has always been a well-defined embarkation between youth and manhood. There, until recent times, when the boy reached an age of ability, the father would make him a pair of long leather pants, his first such garment. From that day, the young man could go forth with responsible position in the village. He could hunt, marry and take a trade. He had no need to doubt his manhood. Every culture has had its pairs of long pants to give its youth.

We have lost these signposts of maturity and invented instead a thing called adolescence. A state of suspended animation during which men find ways to stay fixated in immaturity. Today we often remain in this adolescent womb into our late thirties and even forties. Our cultural legacy to the one unifying masculine element in all of human history, the rite of passage from youth to adulthood, sits in a violet haze along with the Edsel. We all lose...except of course, the breweries.

As I sat and watched my son turning twenty-one, a part of me was saddened because I could not give him his first pair of long pants.

Another part of me was mad as hell!

*Sometimes I cannot tell the difference
between the little boy inside,
and the man in the mirror.*

TURNING FIFTY

I had always dreaded this one. I remember when I was a kid and my relatives turned fifty and had a big party and everyone looked so old. It's amazing how fifty doesn't look nearly as old as it used to. Well I'm fifty today. Somehow though, the world seems much the same as it did at twenty. A little smaller perhaps but, with regard to my experience of myself, little appears to have changed. Well, maybe one thing. Sometimes I get this strange sense of a fourteen year-old boy trying to sneak out from behind my left ear. Or is it the right? Never mind. I still have the same 33 inch waist I did when I was twenty, and I haven't noticed my height shrinking any. My hair, wavy at thirty, waved goodby at forty. There is no remorse there...well, perhaps a little.

Now that I think of it though, I guess I don't move quite as fast as then. The wonderful, exciting young girls are just as wonderful and exciting as ever. Especially to my fourteen year- old. (I call him Patrick.) Patrick doesn't seem to miss a single one (the wonderful, exciting young girls), and he just delights in their highly visible forms. But as a mature man, I couldn't possibly let him expose his joy, could I? I'd get arrested for sure 'cause the world can't see him. Only I can see him. We do have a lot of fun together, and you can be sure that the old saying is true: A man never gets too old for a twenty-one year- old girl.

Fourteen is a perfect age for Patrick. He has developed the intelligence and vocabulary to talk to me, but not the independence to be out on his own. I still must father him, and God knows, I need the practice. But he is not the same as either of my two own boys when they were fourteen. They were nerds in a way. Patrick is wiser, much wiser. He is more of a friend, you might say. Often, I find I go to him for advice rather than the other way around, which you may think is the way it should be. For instance, he's the one who advised me to buy the motorcycle. I ride it all the time now. Cars are OK, but we love the bike. On my own, I would never have thought to do that, and look at the fun I would have missed. Ride'n down the coast at 2:00 a.m. in the cold March California fog, the old guy driving was nearly frost bitten, but Patrick, he was singing love songs. What a guy!

When the business gets heavy and the old guy starts thinking about an afternoon nap, it's Patrick that comes up with the Yo-Yo, and demands that I practice "walking the dog." When the days get long and gray, he's always the one who offers to buy the pizza and beer.

When my ego has plunged to its lowest depths with some personal defeat, it is Patrick who comes up with the frivolous but life-saving trip to the movies and throws popcorn off the edge of the balcony.

When youngsters attach themselves to imaginary friends, it is often a concern for those parents who have read the pop-psychology books, and of course, the school psychologist. (I am more concerned about those parents; the school psychologists are beyond help.) When adults do it, it can be a delightful private game, as long as the little one doesn't take over. We often hear about dealing with the child within, who represents our insecurities and hidden angers. I think perhaps we might consider spending more time listening to him and laughing with him. Listening to the child within is the latest fad in the therapy field. Oh yes, therapists have fad interests just like real people. The only difference is that therapists take fads seriously. But this one might just hang around awhile.

Patrick has been responsible for getting me through a lot of tough spots. He comes out at those times when I would really like to have a Teddy Bear, but of course my ego would never allow that. I mean, what if someone should see it? He is a constant companion in the car, especially on long trips. We have good talks. We remember a lot of things about the days when I was his age and I get to see how far I've really come; to measure my growth.

As men we don't get much acknowledgement from our world. We struggle along and find our values in material things that can be counted, lit up, polished or will lick our face. But Patrick knows. He can tell me all the things I need to hear and, at the end of a long hard day, stuck in traffic and hungry, he never fails to find a way to make me laugh. Sometimes he's the only joy available for miles.

In twenty years I'll be seventy, and I can't help but wonder if Patrick will grow up too. Geez, I hope not. Fourteen is a perfect age, and I sure would miss him.

THE PRISONER

It was just another perfect day in San Diego. The sun was shining, the weather warm and dry. The radio talk show was chattering on about this and that as I drove along the freeway. My mind, miles away in some other dimension, was suddenly awakened when I heard, **"... at least thirty percent of all prisoners in the state penitentiary system never get a visitor during the term of their incarceration."** I turned up the radio and listened intently as the representative of a national organization of outreach volunteers talked about their program.

I had been active in men's issues for several years, but prisons and the people who populate them had never been one of my things. But this day something inside me clicked on, and what hit me was I somehow couldn't care less what a man did--I could not see anyone spending years behind bars without a single visitor. We are, after all, human beings - not animals.

The uniformed man in the front of the room said, "... the only difference between you and the prisoner is that you made a few different choices. There I was, in the Donovan State Penitentiary, in San Diego, getting a briefing on the rules before I met "my prisoner." If you've never been in a penitentiary before, it is a most unnerving experience. Double walls of chain link fencing twelve feet high, topped with three foot circumference razor wire coils, everywhere you go. Guards with guns at every corner. Real guns--loaded guns. Those guys are serious about keeping the prisoners in. One gets the idea they're not nuts about visitors either.

I sat at a small round table and watched the others as I waited for Joe to come down to the visitors' area. Lonely, angry men spending a few precious moments with girlfriends, wives and babies. I couldn't believe how many babies there were. At the next table a young man in blue denim brushed his wife's long, satin black hair in malignant silence, as their infant slept on the table in its car seat. Around the room the others played cards or dominoes. Young boys ran unattended around the room, not knowing how to relate to the strange men in blue they called "father." These men who could not look their sons and daughters in the eye through the guilt and shame.

As he approached the table I stood up and introduced myself. He had waited over a year for an assigned match (friend.) He was black, big and not very pretty. This was, in fact, the ugliest man I had ever seen. Enough scars on his head to write a horror movie around. He was nervous, about as nervous as I was. At twenty-six he had no front teeth and he walked with a knife-induced swagger that was almost a limp. He had lived many more than twenty-six years.

It took me about fifteen minutes to open him up. When I finally did he cried. Never had I seen a man in so much emotional pain. To have a visitor, even an older white man, was like the coming of Christ to this man, at that moment. We talked.

I was leaving, standing in line with the other visitors waiting for the chain link door to slowly whine open, letting us out to a small yard. We entered the yard, the gate grinding closed behind us. We found ourselves locked in a twelve foot high chain link room. We stood there for perhaps ten minutes until the bus drew up. I noticed that I was the one man in a crowd of about fifty women and children. One man visiting one man. I had never felt so lonely. I knew at that point how Joe felt.

Why were there no men visiting other men? Where were the fathers, the brothers, the uncles?

As time went on and the visits came regularly, we both became more comfortable. It was not an easy trip for me. It was about an hour's drive each way. Another forty-five minutes to process in and a half hour to process out, and I only got an hour with him for all of that. The system is designed to dehumanize and humiliate. Humiliation is the name of the game in prison. The guards are well trained in the process and it doesn't stop with the prisoners. There is an attitude.

Joe was up for the third time. The conviction was for attempted murder. I never asked him for the details. It didn't matter. I saw a Joe I doubt anyone else in the world knows. Why he consented to drop his guard with me I do not know. I found him to be one of the most sensitive and caring human beings I have ever known. I know a lot of men who profess vulnerability and sensitivity, but I never met one who felt it more than Joe. I also know, given the numbers of convicted men and the institutional space available, one needs to work hard at getting into a penitentiary today. He is there for good reason, but it doesn't mean he should be forgotten.

Joe will be up for parole in 1995. He is scared to death to get out, but can't stand the thought of another day in jail. He was born in the Los Angeles ghetto, and joined the gang at eleven. He never bothered to go to high school. His entire support system is in the streets of L.A. His blood family gave up on him. He never had a girlfriend. His friends are all dead or in jail or hiding out lest they be either. Every person or condition that ever gave him any level of self-esteem is there in the streets. The fact that there are more young black males in prison today than in college was not lost on him.

When he gets out, according to state law, his choices are clear. He can only go back to his "home." There is no other place. He must return to his home of record to qualify for parole. When he hits the street he has two more clear choices: He can refuse to join the gang and they will kill him...it's automatic...or he can rejoin the gang. If he goes back to the gang he has only two options: Be back in jail within six months and die there, or die in the streets at the hands of the police, another gang, or his own. Barely more than a child, death is all there is for him. I have to keep reminding myself that this is a human being!

But hold on. Perhaps there is more here than it would seem. Joe has taught himself to read, and enjoys it immensely. The fact that the prison library has few books means nothing to him. He just reads the same books over and over. He has practically memorized dozens of Louis L'Amour's western novels. Joe asks questions of himself and of me, which tell me he does not want to die. He wants desperately to find some way out. I would like to help him. I hope that perhaps, by being his friend, I can. But I don't believe it. He refers to himself as a "criminal", which he is of course, but his negative self-image is what he defines himself by in the whole. He sees only that part of himself, rather than that as only a part of his totality. It seems to me there is a part of Joe in each of us but, as the man said, most of us make other choices. If God truly lives in each of us, how can we deny that part of us that is Joe?

The American prison system is an outrageous failure from every perspective possible. The term rehabilitation is no longer even thrown about loosely. There is no rehabilitation there. There is no correction in the departments of correction. There is only time warp. There is only a quagmire which reinforces laws written by politicians struggling to get re-elected by a frightened public; failures of the police, the judicial and social services, and the penal systems. And, because the system is dominated by men and incarcerates primarily men (95% nationally), it is a failure of, for, and by, all men.

We build new prisons at an alarming rate every year. Every city and state budget in the country tries to fund more police at every opportunity. I think it would be a lot cheaper and more effective if more of us made a friend in prison and experienced the joy of being a positive role model to a man who never knew one. Helping a man stay out of prison is far cheaper than supporting him in one, both in terms of dollars and human values.

Ironically, I also get to work with those cops who suffer from severe burnout, post traumatic stress, chronic nervous and mental exhaustion, nightmares, neurotic paranoia, and who can't trust anyone who isn't a cop.

It's very sad...it isn't right...but its very real.

PROLOGUE TO THE RAVEN - 1962 A.D.

As the first joints of my tattered and bleeding fingers reached the top edge of the canyon rim, boot toes dragging lifelessly behind my numbed knees, I yelled with a dry, exhausted crackle, "We made it!" Tom was a hundred yards behind, also on all fours. The news gave him sudden strength and he stood, starting to move at a barely functional pace toward me and the top.   Seventeen hours earlier we had entered the Grand Canyon, never dreaming that the 50-some degrees at the top would become 115 at the bottom.   And Christ, who needed water anyway? It sure didn't look *that* far down.

I lay on the edge of the rim and looked back into the leaded darkness and couldn't quite believe we were still alive. City boys don't handle the fear that mother nature harbors very well.   The fright and the death symbol of that canyon experience would leave it's mark deep in my unconscious for 25 years.

Less than a month earlier, sitting on a cold rock along the shore of Long Island sound in southern Connecticut, this trip west had become a commitment to ourselves and each other that was not to be changed. In that now far-off dream, the cool breeze and the night's third joint made it as much a part of my life as the bloodied and filthy hands that I now looked down on. "It was worth it, worth every second of it" I said silently, but had no idea why,...

That trip to the Colorado River a mile below and back up, at the age of twenty-two, was one of the few true rites of passage in my life. That was the day I crossed over into manhood with a meaning far beyond my awareness, but one that would come back to visit years later as I became able to understand. It took much too long.

Prologue to the Raven - 1962 A.D.

Tom and I went on to California. The plan was to spend the summer sleeping on the beach, screwing hundreds of California girls and getting high. Tom lasted a week and got a ride back east. I got a room at a fraternity house at UCLA for a dollar a day with kitchen privileges, screwed a couple of eastern girls who had come west to meet California guys, and got high on the smog on the way to collect my unemployment check each week. All in all, it wasn't much of a summer. But it was 1962. The draft buildup had taken a sharp turn upward and John Kennedy had said the mess in the jungles of the Far East would be over in a few months.

Dropping out of college to spend a year in the west was a dream come true. What I hadn't counted on was being promptly draft reclassified and offered a chance to become part of the war effort. In late August, I joined the Army to live through my second rite of passage.

THE RAVEN - 1987 A.D.

For centuries the Native American has known that the human being comes into life not knowing certain things; and that certain other things cannot be learned by choice. Some things must be given to humankind by Spirit if we are to have them at all, and it is up to Spirit to decide when such knowledge is to be given. Discovery of the masculine spirit is one of these gifts. Seeking the masculine spirit is particularly difficult during these times of rapid human transition. It is the job of the seeker to make himself available to Spirit for the work to be done.

Over the years, I have given myself up to Spirit on many occasions for the purpose of receiving certain knowledge, and have never been disappointed. Even when I did not receive what I thought I wanted, I did get what I needed. This has been particularly true of the solitary vision quest. This spiritual and nearly exclusive male practice is encountered historically in many native societies worldwide. The most frequent reference to the vision quest is the Native American practice of going deep into the solitude of wilderness to seek the vision of one's life purpose, guide animal, or whatever shows up.

It was one such quest twenty-five years prior in the Grand Canyon of Arizona that brought me closer to death and to life at the same time than I had ever been. And it was here I was to find my guide animal. I had never been sure I would have a guide animal, or that I even wanted one. With two cats and a dog at home, it really didn't seem necessary. But the guide animal comes to a different home.

For most men there are times in life in which the risk of losing everything becomes a major motivating force...at times almost mystically irresistible. This is something that women find impossible to understand about us. It is something we men don't have a clue about, and yet, find relentlessly tempting. It has been written about by poets and philosophers and story tellers throughout history without resolution. We will sacrifice, often in a single moment's decision, years of sweat and planning for some bizarre, often indistinguishable yearning. We will give up years of training in a given field to play music or open a restaurant. We walk out on twenty years of marriage to find a younger woman who will do the same things we hated our long time wives doing. We jump from airplanes and bungee cords, ride ever faster cars and motorcycles. We break law after law and set ever greater standards of violence.

But as all coins have two sides, there is another side to this risk-taking that can open great new vistas of understanding. The one I wish to describe is the vision quest.

To anyone who has been to the Grand Canyon I need not explain the almost unfathomable immensity of this hole. Given an opportunity, the canyon will bring up every emotion the human being is capable of: Every fear, every nightmare, every love and sweet dream. It has the power to bring a man face to face with his soul. But hanging over the steel guard rails along the south rim vistas is only an introduction to the magnificent lady. Climbing down into her belly and experiencing her sheer beauty, majesty and loneliness is metaphorically speaking, spiritually orgasmic.

I had mounted this spirited lady of the night only once before.

That time she nearly killed me. I was twenty-one then. Foolish enough to go into her in late June without water, and young and strong enough to make it out, seventeen grueling hours later on my hands and knees, dangerously dehydrated, exhausted and thoroughly beaten. For twenty-five years I lived with the need to get even for that horrendous defeat of my masculinity. I would have been well-advised to quit while I was ahead. Fortunately I wasn't.

The trip from Flagstaff to the canyon should have warned me. I had never seen such rain in my life. I was forced to drive the motorcycle into the Kaibab forest and cover it and me with a poncho and just sit for hours in the violence until the thunder and lightning broke and allowed me to resume the journey. It was dark when I arrived at the rim, so I pitched my tent alongside the road for the night. At sunup I headed for the trail I had chosen to conquer for my quest. The Hermit's trail.

I parked the bike on the edge of an old abandoned paved lot, detached my gear and locked it up. The tourists loaded and unloaded from the buses at the Hermit's Rest visitors center two hundred yards away, smoking cigarettes and chasing children. No one even thought about coming this way. Built in the early 1900's by the Santa Fe Railroad Company, the trail was abandoned in 1932. Its fame comes from the fact that it is the end of the line for the tour buses that travel the South rim. I lifted the forty-four pound pack onto my back and headed for the weathered old sign that now only ghostly suggested "trailhead." The drop-off from parking lot to canyon mouth is soul wrenching. I stepped forward into the breast of my seductive mistress.

It wasn't long before I discovered I had made the unforgivable hiker's error of neglecting to cut my toenails before starting my descent on the ancient, unmaintained trail. The drop to Hermit's Rapids was intense and in places ran to 45 degrees on boulders the size of basketballs. Although the temperature at the rim was about sixty degrees on the early morning departure, it increased at the rate of about ten degrees an hour and registered 110 by 11:00 a.m. The trail disappeared under avalanches of rock so often I stopped counting. Within thirty minutes of descent the front edge of my boots had shoved the nails on both large toes deep into their cuticles. The toes quickly became blistered and infected. By the time I came to a place where I could stop and cut the nails it was too late. The constant downward pressure of my 180 pounds plus the pack had done its damage. My socks were stained red with blood. The trip had just begun.

If you want to find the meaning of life, hike down into that void for about six hours and suddenly notice that you are no longer on a marked trail. Looking down you see a sheer cliff leading 2,000 feet down to nothing but more rock. No place to get to and no way to get there. So you look back thinking, "Well, I'll just follow the trail back and start over when it becomes clearer." Suddenly you see the same thing behind as forward. The trail has simply disappeared. Miles from the rim, miles from the river. You are perhaps the first person to be here in several years. You begin to look for skeletons.

Walking a trail such as this is an enormous challenge and will test the mettle of one's manhood or womanhood severely. Individually, the difficulty of the climb, the heat or the pain would each have been manageable. The combination would have challenged Steven King.

Canyon thunderstorms can be nature at her most magnificent. I encountered three of them by the halfway point. My conversations with Spirit were becoming unpublishable, even in this day of liberal fourth estate freedoms. When the third storm began to swell and pillow overhead, I had been walking for six hours. My thermometer read 121 as I rounded the last series of switchbacks leaving the magnificent Cathedral Stairs formations. Soon a warm rain started to fall in solid sheets and the trail turned into a river of mud and stone. The blistering sun had moved across the void, sitting outside the clouds, taunting me mercilessly from the north rim. After a few minutes of tortuous chaos, it was replaced by a misty gray fog of diffused darkness, and steam rose from the hot rocks like an eerie horror movie. Then another round of chaos would repeat. It was like living inside a Salvador Dali painting. I stumbled and slipped along, singing old New England seafaring songs, my determination still high but my senses dulled by the pain and the rain and the fatigue. Occasionally a lightning bolt would shatter my manufactured reality as it careened across the sky from one cloud to another. The thunder that followed was like being caught between the cannons in the 1812 Overture. I wondered how the canyon could have survived this pounding for all these billions of years.

Then, as I turned a corner along a ridge of red sandstone, I spotted ahead a cavern alongside the trail. It was a low, dry horizontal shelf, about three feet deep into the rock and just large enough for a man my size to slip into and lie safely and securely until the rain stopped. As I approached, a raven hopped lightly to the open edge, stared at me for just a moment and flew out. The collected debris indicated that it had been often used as a similar refuge for the canyon wildlife. I swept away the light brush and dried feces, climbed in, and drifted through time-space into a welcome, restful sleep. As I closed my eyes for the last time I caught a glimpse of the raven sheltered under a nearby scrub Juniper. He just sat and stared at me, pissed, I thought, for stealing his shelter. After a while the storm spent its violence and disappeared, the sun broke through, and within minutes the desert resumed its dry, barren splendor. I eased myself out of the protection of the cave-shelf and, with newly rested determination, continued my walk to the old campsite, an hour or so beyond which was the wild Colorado River. A short distance away I turned back to look humbly at the caves, thanking Spirit for the gift.

I spent that first night in fever, too weary to care much about anything. The next morning the fever broke and I felt well enough to hike to the rapids. There I spent the day repairing myself and journaling the dreams from the cave. That night the sky became a perfect canvas. It was what Michelangelo must have seen when he looked up at the stark, empty ceiling of the Sistine Chapel with charcoal in hand. I painted my dreams.

The following morning the pain and fever returned. I was too miserable to stay the planned four days, and saddened that I would fail to gain my vision. I packed up and prepared to leave for the rim. It was gray and hot again and I watched the clouds forming their poetry against the backdrop of tan, red, and white rock and blue sky. It seemed reasonable that I could easily reach the shelter of the cave again long before nightfall and from there complete my journey gently up the walls of barren stone to the top by noon the next day.

Lifting the pack onto my back, I noticed the raven again. He was an unusually large bird of intense, almost transparent, glossy blackness. He had followed me from the cave and spent the days and nights just out of reach at my campsites. I assumed he was there to share my rations, but I was fasting this trip and, having nothing to share, I was quite surprised to see him still around. We talked quite a lot as I sat on the rocks, soaking my feet in the soothing ice cold foam of the Colorado rapids, reading to him from my journal. He allowed himself to sit just far enough away from me that I could not touch him, but close enough that we could lock our gazes upon each other, disturbed only by an occasional blink. He got quite a bit more information from me than I from him, nevertheless, it was nice to have a friend. I bid him farewell and started the now dreadfully painful trip up.

Walking on, I watched as the raven would fly ahead, circle, land on a suitable brush limb and wait for me to reach him. It was as though the bird knew just how far I could walk before needing to take a rest. Each time I stopped I'd look up, and there he would be. Then I noticed he seemed to time the rests. After a period, he would cackle and caw, flap his wings and fly up a short ways. When I got up and began to walk he would quiet down, take flight, circle and pick another rest spot. I don't know exactly when I realized that he was symbolically taking my hand and leading me up to the rim, step by step along the sheer drops, blind walls and disappearing trail.

The storms came up late this day. The sun was getting ready to set, which one had to surmise from the color of the sky since it can't be seen after mid-afternoon from the depths of the cavern. I was puzzled because I should have passed the cave long before that time. Not only did I not see the cave, but even the formidable rock formations the cave was in, seemed to have disappeared. I ended up pitching my tent right over the trail which was sloped at a thirty degree angle and just wide enough for my sleeping bag. One of the tent's corners hung off a precipice several hundred feet high. I cannot now imagine a worse place to camp, but at the time I welcomed it.

By this time the fever had taken control of me and I do not remember a great deal more about the trip up. I concentrated on my raven and put my life in his hands. He asked that I surrender my desire to control what was happening and simply trust that he would lead me to safety. He guided me skillfully across the pathless avalanches and never-ending switchbacks. We passed not a single other human being. Raven became my world. Never, however, did I forget the unsettling question of what had happened to the cave.

Many hours later we crossed the last turn and I climbed up to the paved lot and sat down on a boulder. Raven was perched in an old scrub oak growing out of a crack in the ancient blacktop, about twenty-five feet away. We sat in silent communion for several moments. Then, quietly, he settled down on the rock next to me, within inches of my battered body. We said our goodbyes and he took flight, circled three times above me and disappeared back into the canyon, effortlessly surfing a downdraft.

After many days of contemplation I became aware of a number of things. First, my Raven was given to me to guide me through the rest of my life. He has often done so since that trip into my spirit womb. Second, there are no caves on the Hermit Trail. And yet they were there. They did shelter and protect me. They remain as much a part of my reality as are my arms and legs. My masculine logic tells me it was all a dream. But I know that Spirit is wondrously powerful. I also know that in order to truly experience my masculine self, I must meet Spirit face to face. I need only to be willing to have the experience.

Where does the friendship go
when the friend is gone?

MUSH, WHERE ARE YOU?

Each gender of course, has its idiosyncrasies at various ages. Teenagers of any age or gender cease, for the most part, to be human for the greater part of that stage of life. They seem to take on some unrecognizable form that only Art Buchwald and Steven Spielberg are able to deal with. Male children between the ages of ten and thirteen are, however, distinctly unique in the way in which they view the world. Such was the case with me and Mush.

Martin, or Mush as he was painfully but universally known, was my friend. The moniker came as an aberration of his Hebrew name "Moisha" and the fact that he carried substantially more weight than was appropriate for his frame...he was fat. We contrasted dramatically. I was probably ten inches taller and weighed half as much. It was at eleven that I got my first pair of glasses, and when I first met Mush. We became a classic, nerd twosome in the tradition of Laurel and Hardy, but we did great things for our country.

The Korean War was in the news regularly, so we decided to do our part and join the Civil Air Patrol. Joining was a bit of a drag because we wanted guns and ammo and walkie-talkies, but all we got was a little card for our wallets. But never mind. We went down to the local Army-Navy surplus store and bedecked ourselves in white M.P. belts and canteens, and those little white, round WWII Navy sailor caps upon whose vertical sides we laboriously lettered "CIVIL AIR PATROL". A significant part of me wants to go hide even now as I realize we actually went to school with those get-ups on. We thought everyone would be insanely jealous, and girls would love us.

No wonder we were always getting beat up.

The amazing thing was, we couldn't figure it out then. Mush and I were inseparable for two years. We did our homework together. We sipped cherry cokes at the fountain in the local drug store, arguing about what next year's new cars would look like. We looked at dirty magazines whenever we could find them. We discovered our sexuality together. We sought the wondrous secrets hidden beneath girls' sweaters together and spent endless hours pondering them.

One of the reasons I became friends with Mush in the first place was that they had one of the few TV sets in the neighborhood. In the early days of TV, wrestling was a big attraction. We watched wrestling on TV with his mother, who was a world authority on the subject and never missed a match. She even took us downtown to watch it live at the Knights of Columbus Hall from time to time. She was also very overweight and the first woman I had ever known with a mustache. Mush's Mom was also one of those delightfully entertaining people who could vicariously experience the pain of the wrestlers. Every move, every slam, every twist was her own. She vocalized it so as to cause windows to shake and shutters to slam shut and no doubt, neighbors to move.

I don't remember much about Mush's Dad. I think he prayed a lot and the only time I ever saw him was watching the wrestling.

Anyway, after the eighth grade, Mush went to Hebrew High to become a rabbi, and I went on to Central High to become confused. I don't know how successful Mush was, but I sure did create my goal. I never saw Mush again, not even accidentally at McDonald's or anything. Some time after high school started, he moved and I moved and we lost track. In those days people didn't move like we do today. Even if someone moved a few blocks away or across town, it was like moving to another country, and we separated ways.

By the time my own boys hit seven or eight, they delighted in hearing stories about my youth. I guess that's pretty normal. Dads are very much anomalies to their kids, and it helps a boy develop his sense of relationship to Dad and to himself to hear that Dad was once the same as he is. I always tried to tell them stories that happened to me at whatever age they were at the time. That process, in fact, had a lot to do with my developing an appreciation for the art of story telling. The day came eventually when Mush came into my mind during one of these story sessions. The name "Mush" so impressed my boys that they never let me forget him again. Every so often as they grew older, if I had a problem, one or other of them would say something like, "Well, what would Mush do?", or " Why don't you call Mush?" and then roll on the floor in belly-busting laughter. They seemed to like the idea of Mush, and I guess each created his own image of him.

All of this, eventually, brings me to a point. I recently read a book about the life of one of America's great millionaires. A man who built incredible monuments in great cities, and was on a first-name basis with all the political officials, mayors, governors, presidents. He built a great hotel in New York City and lived on five floors of it, they say. But he is also described as a friendless man. One who would come home in the wee hours of the morning and sit alone, his wife in a separate bedroom, with only his money to count. I am not against wealth. As others have said, I have been poor and I have been rich and rich is definitely better. But I can't help think, as strange a friendship as Mush and I had, it was something to be treasured. I feel deep concern for a man who has dedicated his life to money, but has not a single fat little kid for a friend. As men, I think we hunger at deep levels for intimacy with other men, for a male friend to cry with, to exorcise our fears and troubles to another man who will not judge us, but will simply listen and tell us it's O.K.

It's been nearly forty years since I last saw Mush, but our friendship lives on in the depths of my memory. That memory is behind my appreciation of all those men I can today, call my friends and those who have been in my life over the years.

If there is a meaning of any kind to life, perhaps it is in the friendships we make along the way.

Mush, if you're out there anywhere, I hope you remember too.

The world provides me
with ample fantasies to play in,
but I get too old and too busy
too quickly to see them.

ONCE UPON A TIME THERE WAS THIS FAIRY PRINCESS...

The invitation to go to Russia to present a workshop on men and men's issues came unexpectedly. Arriving on the day after the ill-fated coup in August of 1991 was an experience I shall never forget. Having lived through our own cultural revolutions of the sixties, I felt a certain deja vu as we stood with the crowds at the barricades in front of the parliament building in Moscow, entrapped by the energy and holding up the old imperial flag Iwo Jima style for our camera-toting "comrades." I also felt a deep compassion and empathy with those brave Russian men and women who had simply decided that their lives could not continue in the patterns of the past seventy-four years. I shared the tears of freedom with those who tended the bonfires and kept vigilant watch as the demonstrations waned and the heaps of flowers offered to the memory of those killed grew deeper. I was deeply touched by the sincerity of the Russian people who were thrilled that we cared enough to be there with them.

I was to present four one-day workshops in Novosibirsk in central Siberia, the eighth largest city in Russia. Few Americans have ever heard of it, but it is a wonderful city full of wonderful people and storybook architecture. The night before the workshop, in a way that can only happen in Russia, I was told that I would be doing one four-day workshop instead. Ten minutes before the doors opened I met my interpreter. I spoke not a word of Russian and the audience spoke the next best thing to no English. I had never worked with an interpreter before, and my world was caving in at a supersonic rate. She stood in front of me and stretched out her young hand in stiff bravado. "Halloo," said she. "Oy vey," said I. We sat down in front of twenty-some therapists from many areas of the country, each waiting for the brilliance that was sure to come with my words. I knew I would be sick.

Her name was Oksana. I did not notice it until later that first day, but she had those uniquely Siberian eyes, the color of deep glacial water that could pierce metal. I noticed quickly that she was the first Russian woman I had met who didn't smoke. I found out almost as quickly that she was brilliant.

As we became more comfortable in the translation and presentation process, I began to notice a number of things about this woman. She was extraordinarily lovely. She sat chair to chair with me throughout the workshop, legs, arms shoulders touching frequently. She translated my words simultaneously and our voices soon blended into a comfortable and natural flow. As the group responded she whispered the translations, her lips only inches from my ear. Her voice had a wonderfully melodic flow, and her accent, I began to discover, was eloquently seductive. I began to notice a strange feeling along the right side of my neck. A warm, happy feeling. Occasionally I would find myself staring at her looking for specific meaning during some difficult moments of communication. It was at these moments that I would lose my concentration and begin to babble on. Fortunately, Russians take babble seriously.

I noticed how her hair grew out of her scalp, the gentle flowing shape of her ear, her perfect, smooth skin, the way her collars wrapped around her neck, and more. But most of all,

I noticed her voice. Well-formed sounds and thoughtful hesitancies as her brain rushed around the syntaxes of two languages, struggling to make sense--her meter and pitch perfect. I also noticed she was exactly half my age. It soon became necessary for me not to look at her lest I get sucked down into the depth of those eyes and lose track completely of my work.

The energy told me I was not lost on her either. We were both on our best behaviors, but I suspect that it was far more difficult for me. Anyway, the workshop was well received and I left feeling deeply rewarded for the experience. Oksana and I said goodbye on the auditorium steps, but we meant a lot of other things. I stood on the steps, watching her for a few moments. Fifty yards or so away she stopped, turned around, and saw me watching her. We waved and, it seemed, touched again for the last time. She haunted my thoughts for months. Well, two months anyway.

One day, just after Thanksgiving, my phone rang. Oksana was in San Francisco translating for some Russian big shot and wanted to come down to see me in San Diego. Oy vey!

We spent a dream day. I drove her around San Diego which is one of America's and certainly the world's loveliest cities. We had a quiet and friendly dinner together, and she stayed overnight in my apartment. We did not as much as touch, outside of a few (too few) hugs. The next morning she left. I drove her to the airport and she just flew away. Dasvadonia, my sweet child.

The story is not the story. The story is what went on with me over this story. I was in a relationship at the time with a wonderful woman who left me with no desire or need to seek out another, and being a naturally monogamous type, I liked it that way. But the connection between Oksana and me had been so strong that my priorities became shaded for about a month after she left. I was fifty-two, Oksana was twenty-six. I was a divorced American in America with a grown family and a girlfriend and was very content with my life. She was a divorced Russian in Russia with a three year-old daughter and a boyfriend. It was impossible. But even now, months later, I can occasionally hear her voice whispering those lilting, gentle sounds in my ear. And if I dare see those eyes in my mind, I'm off in the clouds again, on a flight of fancy.

I think fantasy adds a lot to life. I enjoy a rich and bountiful fantasy life. I find men don't spend enough time in fantasy. We are so busy being busy or bored that we miss the delightful opportunities that exist for us in our creative mind. There is a forest of make-believe available to us that can help make reality far more pleasant. We encourage our kids to listen to the fairy tales of childhood but we become too sophisticated to do it ourselves. We have denied our inherited mythology and have replaced it with none of our own. Whenever possible, I encourage the men I work with to become familiar with the possibilities that exist in fantasy as a way of dealing with and appreciating reality. Life is just too complex to take too seriously. It'll make you crazy.

I shot John Kennedy.

A STORY RETOLD

Once upon a time there was a kingdom, far, far away which was so very deep in the woods that no one on the other side of the woods even knew it existed. Not only that, the people who lived in this kingdom had no idea that the woods ever ended and believed, therefore, that they were the only people in the world. They believed, in fact, that their land was the whole world. There was only one village in this land, and although it was quite large with many families living there, it always seemed that whenever a new baby was born, one of the elders would pass on to worlds beyond the clouds. The storytellers told of the agreement between Eagle and Bear that there was a perfect number of people who could live well in this land, and they would never grow beyond that perfect number.

For many generations the old storytellers had passed down tales of how the great Eagle and great Bear met in a thunderous sky and mated, giving birth to the first ancient cousins of the people of the village. Everyone in the village loved each other because they were all related in some way to the ancient Eagle and the ancient Bear. Each person honored the other and there was no fear or anger and no trespass. When the snows came, the children made sleds of the bark of the great trees that had fallen in the nearby woods and slid joyously down the trails which were cleared unnumbered years before by their fathers' fathers' fathers, and many fathers before them. When the warm summer breezes blew gently across the many lakes surrounding the village, the fathers watched in quiet pride as their sons pulled fish from the nets and spears. The sons followed the fathers behind the plows and wondrous fruit and food and flowers were grown. And the mothers and daughters observed the men, while they too filled their days with love and happiness.

There were many joyous times, as the ancients had wisely set down days for celebration. There were days celebrating the planting of the crops, the harvest, and the feast. There were also special days to celebrate the times when boys and girls became men and women, and the carefree days of youth flowed into mature responsibilities, and each became an important working part of the village. There were many secrets among the women about such things, and, although it was always quite evident when the village girls passed into womanhood, there were few such obvious changes in the boys. Great Eagle and Great Bear had wisely foreseen such problems and planned a special ceremony for the boys so that all would know when boy became man, and all could share in his pride of passage.

For many centuries the village prospered. The elders left to make room for the new. The snow always fell in winter, and the fish grew big for each summer's catch. The boys and girls became men and women, mated, and started the story over again.

Everyone was happy, there was plenty of everything for everyone, and there was joyous ceremony for each birth, each death and each marking of growth.

Then one day there appeared at the edge of the woods a handsome young man on a great white horse, whom no one had ever seen before. He looked much the same as the village folk, although his clothes were strangely different. As he came close to the village, crowds of people gathered around him, for he certainly was a curiosity. He spoke a most frightening sound when trying to speak and seemed deaf to the inquiries of the villagers as to his circumstances. One young man grasped hold of the ropes that guided the wonderful horse of no color and led him to the village leader.

The leader was a wise and aged woman who had lived many winters longer than most. As the lad who had led the stranger there related his story, the old woman seemed to lose the color of life in her leathery face. She quickly dispersed the villagers and directed the visitor into her rooms. For many days and nights the two remained cloistered within the earthen walls of the leader's home. The oil lantern burned long into darkness, and their voices could be heard bouncing across the morning dew.

Finally on the fourth day, just before the sun danced across the western tree tops, the two emerged from the leader's home and walked into the square that was so often used to mark important times. It took only moments for the villagers standing in the square to gather around and form a huge circle.

When all had gathered, as if by prearrangement, the old lady spoke. She told of a new land on the other side of the woods from which the stranger had journeyed. He had become lost while on a hunt and, after many days of travel had discovered the village. She spoke of many wondrous things in the stranger's land, but warned that these were things for the stranger and his cousins to know and not for the people of this village. She said that there was much for the stranger to wonder at in this village also, but not to have for himself. Soon the stranger mounted his horse and headed toward the woods to find his trail home.

Some weeks after the appearance of the stranger, the village leader passed on to the clouds beyond. Her final words were filled with deep concern for her people and she offered a grave warning: "Do not disturb the Eagle and the Bear in their eternal rest," she said. Then she parted.

Well, as you may have guessed a yearning began to beat in the hearts of many of the young men in the village to travel to this forbidden place of the stranger. Indeed, when the stranger finally returned to his own village and told of his adventure, a desire to see this new place also sprang wild among the other men, and each village began to see more new strangers. Soon the young boys found young girls in their visits and married and mated, and took new language, thoughts and customs to each village.

As the years passed, and generation succeeded generation, the customs no longer seemed to fit the needs of the people of either village. Commerce developed and more villages were discovered and further integrated into a common language and thought.

Eventually there came a time when the young boys no longer fished with their fathers, as there was too much work to be done to support the commerce, and the young boys just got in the way. The snow that once covered sledding runs now fell on well-travelled roads, much too busy and dangerous for children to play on. Jealousy and selfishness found ready ground on which to grow as each village had developed its own unique ways of living and concepts of value. Some thought other's things were better than their own, wanted them, and took them. Wars broke out, young boys, particularly, died. The balance of young and old began to wither, and everything seemed to be out of balance. Gone were the ceremonies that gave strength and comfort to the questions of the young and meaning to the old. No longer did the young look to the old for answers and guidance, for no longer was there wisdom to be found there. No longer did the old look to the young for eternal hope, for they had none. Most of all, however, the boys no longer knew when they became men, and therefore could not act as men. The girls no longer looked longingly towards them, for these girls knew not what was expected of them. The boys and the girls quarrelled greatly.

The villages grew into towns, the towns into great cities, and the woods disappeared. Many wonderful things came to be, but prices were paid. The commerce laid waste to the lands, and the fruits thereof declined in number and reward. One city stretched into the next, the young men traveled further and further to find young girls to mate with, and eventually all the traditions and ceremonies of all the people had become no traditions for any of the people.

Great Bear and Great Eagle watched the unfolding of these conditions from beyond the clouds with great sadness, for there was little they could do. They had done the best they could when starting their family, and the winds had done the rest.

There is no end to this story. The ending has been given to each of us to write ourselves. Great Eagle and Great Bear have turned their heads that they may not see what the cousins have done.

It is now up to the cousins.

Who am I?

he sat on the mountain top
and looked out
over the endless landscape
stretching before him.

Who am I?

no one answered.

but millions
heard the question.

AFTERWORD

In nearly every encounter I have with groups of men, I hear comments and words of wisdom that are stories in themselves. I think it a fitting close to offer you, the reader a few of these comments in unedited form. Comments which didn't make it into the story format for this book, but which nonetheless are a large part of it. They are moments in time from the lives of real men; rituals in every sense of the word, which are part of their very sacred and very private worlds. Moments through which we all find ways to connect with the family of humanity through the sharing of a little bit of ourselves.

"…you know, the only thing I really, actually remember about my father before he left, was once when we went to a carnival. We both had to go to the bathroom. I musta been, I don't know, maybe four. There weren't any kid urinals and I'd never used a grownup urinal before, and my father pointed me into this thing and said, man I'll never forget it, he said, "Fill it up, kid". The enormity of the task was beyond me. I looked at this thing and couldn't believe he wanted me to fill it up. He just looked down at me and laughed, and I guess I realized he was just kidding, but here I am forty years later and that's what I remember about my father. And you know what's crazy? I would have done anything and everything possible to fill that damn thing up for him…and probably still would."
Raphael, workshop participant, 1991.

The father flew in from Hawaii, the son from North Carolina The elder was 64, Jim Jr. 36. They had not seen each other for eight years, but talked by phone nearly every month. The hike with five other pairs of fathers and sons took just under two hours from the trailhead to the campsite deep in the central Arizona mountains. As if connected to a celestial timer, the sun set over the raspberry-colored mountains in the west just as the full moon came up over the eastern range, so big and clear one felt sure he could just reach up and take a piece home with him. The light from setting sun to rising moon seemed equally bright, changing only its reflected hue.

We sat by the campfire and I asked each father and son to tell a story. It was to be the story of the funniest thing each could remember about the other. No two partners told the same story, and in most cases neither remembered the other's memorable highlight. We talked about the perspectives each brought into his story. We talked about what each father and each son learned from the other's story. From these stories they found the issues that they wanted to work on for the next three days in the wilderness.

I got to know these twelve men quickly and deeply through their stories. I told them my funniest father story, and we all laughed: All except Jim Sr. I was the facilitator of this group and the only one without a father or son there. Jim Sr. just looked at me for a time in the defining mountain night silence. After a few moments he said softly that he felt my loneliness for my own sons in this company. And Jim Jr. said the same. And we all realized that we learn of the loneliness of manhood through our fathers. We spent another hour talking of loneliness, until the campfire embers lay twinkling back at the sky full of stars.

Jim Jr. and Jim Sr. still live 5,000 miles apart, but they talk to each other weekly and see each other at least twice a year now. They are not quite as lonely as they had been and, thanks to them, neither am I.

"I'm thirty-seven years old and I've never been married. I've been engaged four times since I was eighteen, and all but one of them I broke off at the last minute. I'm a lawyer and have a great job which pays well and I hate it. My Dad hasn't talked to me since I was arrested for selling coke when I was seventeen. My Mom won't interfere; she says that's just the way he is and to let it be, and if she says something he'll just get mad at her. I can't figure out why I can't make a commitment to anything that will make me happy. Every time I get close I can feel him looking over my shoulder, judging me, but he won't go away. All I want to do is to hear him say he loves me...is there something wrong with that?" **Phil, workshop participant, 1992.**

"...I've been sitting here for two hours hearing you talk about rites of passage and getting madder and madder all that time. I'm in my late forties and the closest thing I ever had to a rite of passage was killing a couple thousand faceless human beings in Nam. I'm the result of no rituals and no initiations and no rites of passage and what I'm feeling is that I've really been cheated and it's pissing me off! My life has been full of the crap we talked about here and I don't like it and I don't like myself very much, but my question is what can I do about it now? It's fine and wonderful to talk about how it should have been, but what the hell do I do with all the shit I'm carrying around in my bag? How do I tell my belly to stop hurting and my nightmares to go away? I want someone to tell me what I can do to make being a man feel like something that is worthwhile getting up to in the morning...the rest of it is all bullshit!" **David, from a workshop, 1990.**

Not too long ago I was guest speaker at a weekly men's group sponsored by a local hospital. This group was made up of eight men, average age estimated at 40, who have come together out of personal crisis, and sought psychiatric care to help them through it. I had just completed writing one of the preceding stories, and I was exceptionally sensitive to the attitudes of these men towards women. I listened carefully to the questions they asked and was reminded once again that the problems these men are dealing with have little to do with women; their thoughts do not revolve around the feminist movement and most have little understanding of where women even fit in their lives. These are men seeking to initiate themselves as men first. Then, and not until then, will they have something to offer women, <u>and they know it</u>! Until I told them, these men were not even aware they were part of a men's movement. They had no idea that after the twelve-week cycle was over (based on insurance limitations) there was additional support available to them. These are not men who can support the women's agenda. They are simply not evolved enough in their own development to know how. The militaristic message that men are receiving from the feminists, no matter how well intended, resembles the very syndrome they are trying to understand. They *want* love, not war. These men are not the exceptions; they are representative of the contemporary masculine condition.

"I was a cop for twenty friggin' years. When I was forty my daughter left home and then two years later my son left. Then I got to see that I didn't have much of a relationship with my wife because I had spent all the years of my marriage working and not really participating with the family. With the kids gone we didn't have much use for each other, I guess. After a couple more years, my wife left and all I had was the damn job. The next year I had my twenty [years] in at age forty-six and had to retire. Nobody likes cops except other cops but they're no fun. I got to know what lonely was real fast. There was no real relationship with the kids, and a fat, middle-aged ex-cop, doesn't do too well at those singles things. If it hadn't been for my grandkids I would have ended it right then. I still don't have much going with my son, but my daughter and her kids kept me alive... Somewhere along the line I figure I missed something, and I'd sure like to find it before I die. I'd like to know that my life was worth living." **Carl, from a workshop, 1992.**

Most of the men who come to my workshops come as a result of frustration with their lives. They see an advertisement or hear about it from their friends. I can always tell the new guys. They crowd into the last row, always at least one empty chair between them, arms folded, slouched low lest someone should actually see them there. By the time the introduction is over they have relaxed somewhat, and by the time sharing starts (always required from the audience) they have begun to listen. When they find there are other men there sharing their own concerns, they unfold their arms and listen attentively.

After the half-time break I invite all the men to move forward to the front rows. Most do.

At the end we usually have an open question-and-answer period. Many of the men come up and join me, sitting on the stage or the floor. It often seems they can't get close enough to hope.

"...it was kind of amazing. I can't remember ever actually having a real drum to beat on. I started out real self-conscious. I figured every other guy at the gathering had been playing drums for years, and that everyone could hear my off-beats and that pretty soon someone would come over and ask me to stop playing...I mean, that's what's always happened in my life, and I guess I just got in the habit of quitting or not getting started in anything I didn't think I could do. But I did this drumming thing. I stayed with it, and after a while I started to get into the rhythm with everybody else. I began to notice that there were lots of guys out of the rhythm, but we just kept at it and one by one they came into it and before long there was sixty-three guys all playing together. It was beautiful. I played for my mom and my dad, my old girlfriends, my wife, my kids, my dog, and finally, even for me. I can't tell you how much stress I left in that damn drum. It felt great." **William, from a men's gathering, 1992.**

"I never thought about shaving every morning as a ritual. I just realized this morning that I never actually "look" at myself in the mirror as I shave...I look at the razor, and that part of my face that I'm shaving but I never look at "me". I tried it this morning and I liked what I saw. It's made me feel better about myself all day." **Victor, from a workshop, 1991.**

ABOUT THE AUTHOR

Ken Byers is a social behaviorist and writer with a primary interest in the cultural development and life experience of men. He is one of only a few men in the country to have earned a doctorate degree in Men's Studies. Ken's first book, **"MAN IN TRANSITION, his role as father, son, friend and lover"** has become a classic, practical reader and guidebook for men beginning to seek their own personal awareness and social connectedness. His background as an industrial designer, business consultant and entrepreneur, gives him a unique perspective on men in our culture.

Dr. Byers runs father and son wilderness relationship tours in the mountains of Arizona and Siberia and is an internationally known speaker and facilitator of seminars and workshops for the general public and business clients. He lives in San Diego, California, not too far from his two sons.

Also available from **JOURNEYS TOGETHER** is the book that started it all, **"MAN IN TRANSITION, his role as father, son, friend and lover"**. This book is a primer for men entering the process of discovery and has been acclaimed nation-wide as a basic book on men's issues. It is being used as a guidebook for both course work and individual life transition for thousands of men seeking personal growth and inner expansion.

ORDER FORM

Please send ____ copies of **"MAN IN TRANSITION"** at $9.95 each, or ____ copies of **"WWTMMA?"** at $12.95, plus $1.00 postage per book to:

Name...

Address...

City..

State.............Zip...

I enclose my check for a total of $__________ . _____ .

ORDER FROM:
Journeys Together, P.O. Box 1254 La Mesa, CA 91944

Also please send information on:

☐ Workshops and Seminars

☐ Audio Cassettes available

☐ Father and Son Wilderness tours

☐ Information on having Dr. Byers speak to my group